hRACh

2005

الأدب

Criminal Case 40/61, the Trial of Adolf Eichmann

PERSONAL TAKES

An occasional series of short books in which noted critics write about the persistent hold particular writers, artists, or cultural phenomena have had on their imaginations.

Criminal Case 40/61, the Trial of Adolf Eichmann

An Eyewitness Account

Harry Mulisch

Translated by Robert Naborn

Foreword by Debórah Dwork

University of Pennsylvania Press

Philadelphia

The translation of this book was made possible with financial support
from the Foundation for the Production and Translation of Dutch Literature.

Originally published as *De Zaak 40/61: Een Reportage*
by Uitgeverij de Bezige Bij, Amsterdam
Copyright © 1961 Harry Mulisch

10 9 8 7 6 5 4 3 2 1

Published by
University of Pennsylvania Press
Philadelphia, Pennsylvania 19104-4011

Library of Congress Cataloging-in-Publication Data

Mulisch, Harry, 1927–
  [Zaak 40/61. English.]
  Criminal case 40/61, the trial of Adolf Eichmann : an eyewitness account /
Harry Mulisch ; translated by Robert Naborn ; foreword by Debórah Dwork.
    p. cm. — (Personal takes)
  Includes bibliographical references and index.
  ISBN 0-8122-3861-3 (alk. paper)
    1. Eichmann, Adolf, 1906–1962. 2. Trials (Genocide)—Jerusalem. 3. War
crime trials—Press coverage—Netherlands. 4. Holocaust, Jewish
(1939–1945). I. Title. II. Series.

DD247.E5M813 2005
364.15′1′092—dc22   2004061167

To **W. L. BRUGSMA,**
on the occasion of ten years of friendship

C O N T E N T S

FOREWORD

Debórah Dwork

"I have to inform the Knesset that a short time ago one of the greatest of the Nazi war criminals, Adolf Eichmann, . . . was discovered by the Israel security services," Prime Minister David Ben Gurion announced to an astonished Israeli parliament on May 23, 1960. He continued: "Adolf Eichmann is already under arrest in Israel and will shortly be placed on trial in Israel under the terms of the Nazi and Nazi Collaborators (Punishment) Law."* Ben Gurion's declaration unleashed a storm. If many Israelis cheered the security service's capture of Eichmann and his removal from Argentina to the Jewish state, Argentinean and American government officials decried what they called an illegal abduction and an infringement on Argentina's sovereignty. The Israelis countered by asking why Argentina had sheltered this war criminal for over a decade, had never extradited any Nazis, and still gave many safe harbor. When the Soviets weighed in reminding everyone that, according to agreements of 1943 and 1945, war criminals were to be tried in the country where they committed their heinous

*Harry A. Zeiger, ed., *The Case Against Adolf Eichmann* (New York: New American Library, 1960), p. 11.

acts, Argentina, the United States, and the UN Security Council grew quiet. Eichmann remained in Jerusalem. Accused of crimes against the Jewish people, crimes against humanity, and war crimes, he was brought to trial on April 11, 1961. Journalists around the world, including Harry Mulisch, saw this as an international event of historic magnitude.

Born March 19, 1906, in Solingen, a town famous for its blades (knives, scissors, surgical instruments), young Otto Adolf Eichmann moved with his family from Germany to Linz, Austria, in 1913. Neither a gifted nor diligent student, Adolf was pulled out of the academic high school by his father. He did not do any better at the vocational school for engineering. His father put him to work in his own modest mining enterprise until he found Adolf a job as a salesman in the Austrian Elektrobau Company in 1925. Perhaps it was there that Eichmann learned how to sell: a talent he would use to his advantage later. Through a family connection, Eichmann got a much better post two years later (1927) as the sales representative for Upper Austria of the Vacuum Oil Company. Perhaps it was through this experience that he learned the value of connections to advance his career: a lesson he never forgot. He did well at the Vacuum Oil Company until he was transferred to the Salzburg office; his performance plummeted and he was fired. But he had a new interest to buoy him. Invited by Ernst Kaltenbrunner, a young lawyer in Linz whose father was friends with Eichmann's father, Adolf joined the NSDAP, the National Socialist People's Party, or Nazi party. At that point, the Austrian Nazi Party did not offer full-time employment. Kaltenbrunner, for example, who became Eichmann's boss in 1942 as chief of the Reich Security Main Office (RSHA), still worked as a full-time attorney in his father's firm. Eichmann therefore moved back to Germany, where the party suggested he train in the military. He accepted with alacrity and went off to two SS (Protection Squads) military camps in Bavaria, where he learned to drill and advanced to the rank of SS-corporal.

Eichmann was moving along, but his real career began a year later (1934) when he applied for a position in the main office of Himmler's Security Service (SD). Headed by Reinhard Heydrich, a former navy intelligence officer, the SD had been established by

Himmler to serve as the intelligence service of the party. Spying on his comrades consolidated Himmler's control over them and the power of his SS organization. Eichmann found a niche as the SS expert on Zionist matters, which included a trip to Palestine to report on the Jewish colonization project. At that point, the Nazis' "solution" to the "Jewish Problem" was emigration. When Himmler decided to centralize the management of Jewish emigration procedures (visas, economic arrangements, transfer of capital), Eichmann took charge of the design and implementation of this streamlined "service."

The new system was never set up in Germany itself but, within days of the Anschluss (annexation) of Austria in March 1938, Eichmann turned up in Vienna to organize the emigration of Jews. His headquarters in a palace stolen from the Rothschild family became the Central Office for Jewish Emigration. As far as Eichmann was concerned, emigration no longer depended upon the initiative of individual Jews. Emigration had become expulsion, an operation supervised by the SD involving officials of the finance ministry, the police, the currency control office, and representatives of the Jewish community. He compared his system to a conveyor belt. "The initial application and all the rest of the required papers are put in at one end, and the passport falls off at the other end," he explained rather proudly when interrogated by Avner Less for trial in 1962. He did not tell the Israeli police captain that the conveyor belt swallowed up the Jews' rights as well as their money and that the passport they received allowing them to leave was valid for a mere fourteen days. Nor did he explain that the system was financed with money taken from the Jews themselves. What he did report was that his Central Office of Jewish Emigration had forced fifty thousand Jews to leave within six months, "a first in the German administrative machine." It made him a star in the Nazi constellation, an attraction for "numerous visitors from various departments in the so-called Old Reich, who came to Vienna for this express purpose."*

*Jochen von Lang with Claus Sibyll, eds., *Eichmann Interrogated: Transcipts from the Archives of the Israeli Police*, trans. Ralph Mannheim (New York: Farrar, Straus, & Giroux, 1983), pp. 52, 56.

For Austria's Jews this conveyor belt was a nightmare. How were those "required papers" Eichmann mentioned so airily to be obtained? The Nazis wanted the Jews to leave. The Jews, humiliated, abused, and terrorized from the first day of the Anschluss, sought to escape. But, as their coreligionists in Germany had learned for five years, emigration was a desperate search for sponsors abroad, tax clearance forms, entry visas, train tickets, and ship berths.

By the time the Germans occupied the Czech lands (March 1939) and Eichmann had been moved to Prague to replicate his success, the Czech Jews found it nearly impossible to get visas. Fearing failure, Eichmann settled upon a reservation for these unwanted people. He explained his plan to Heydrich, who told Himmler, who told Hitler. Eichmann got approval to proceed and, a few weeks later, was promoted to head of Subsection IV (Gestapo)-B (Sects)-4 (Jews) of the RSHA in Berlin. The Germans conquered Poland in September, and their military success invited actualization of Eichmann's new and more violent "solution." He promptly established the Nisko reservation in the Lublin district to which a total of 95,000 Jews were deported. The mortality en route as well as upon arrival was staggering.

As the Germans devoured Europe, they got land they wanted and Jews they didn't. Emigration and reservations as a "solution" to this "problem" no longer sufficed. Eichmann's job was to map the location of Jews throughout Europe and to devise schemes first to move them out of German and German-occupied territories and then, when there was nowhere left to ship Jews, to organize transports to ghettos and camps. He managed brilliantly. Notwithstanding Germany's military defeats starting in 1943, notwithstanding the certain demise of the Third Reich by the time he went to Hungary, home to the last major Jewish community still within Nazi reach, Eichmann carried on deporting Jews to their death. By 1945, Eichmann had been directly involved in the murder of one million Jews and indirectly responsible for the deaths of at least another two million.

After the war, as Harry Mulisch explains in this report, Eichmann made his way south and west. Picked up by the Americans, he slipped out of an internment camp with false papers supplied to him by a clandestine Nazi organization in the camp. Helped by the international neo-Nazi central organization ODESSA and the Catholic Church, Eichmann got to Rome, where the Vatican gave him a refugee pass. Now Ricardo Klement, he obtained a visa for Argentina. And there he lived, with his wife, Vera, and four sons (three born in Germany, the last in Argentina) from July 1952 until Israeli security agents captured him in 1960.

Harry Mulisch was not a journalist at the time. The Israelis had reserved 450 seats for news writers in the courtroom, and Mulisch wished to occupy one. He persuaded the weekly magazine *Elseviers Weekblad* to send him to Jerusalem. It must not have been a difficult decision for the editors: Mulisch was an up-and-coming author whose work they had published before (a short story, "De Kamer"). His first novel, *Archibald Strohalm* (1952), had won the prestigious Reina Prinsen Geerlingsprize for young writers, and he had gone on to publish two collections of novellas (1953, 1957), one book of aphorisms (1958), and three novels (1954, 1956, 1959) to critical acclaim and increasing financial success. And he had an interesting history of his own.

Mulisch's father, Karl Victor Mulisch, was an Austrian officer in World War I. Sent to Belgium, he met his future father-in-law, a German Jewish banker named Schwarz, who worked for a German bank in Antwerp. The banker and his family went to Amsterdam in 1918; K. V. Mulisch returned to Vienna. But postwar Vienna offered little, and Mulisch wrote to Schwarz for a job. He got a position and, in 1926, daughter Alice Schwarz as well. She was eighteen; he nearly twice her age. They had Harry a year later (July 29, 1927) and divorced in 1936, three years after Hitler had come to power in Germany and four years before the occupation of the Netherlands (1940).

Most unusually, Harry remained with his father when his parents divorced. They lived in Haarlem; his mother moved to Amsterdam. This helped to protect Harry when the Netherlands fell to the Germans. According to Third Reich racial definitions, Harry was a "half-Jew" and thus at risk. A "half-Jewish" child living with a Jewish mother would have been targeted for deportation with her. K. V. Mulisch went further, however. A fellow World War I officer who was now, after the Anschluss, a German officer sought out his old friend. Mulisch senior consorted with the enemy: he greeted his former comrade and offered him hospitality. The friend, in turn, got him a job as one of the directors of the notorious Lippmann-Rosenthal bank, which had a key role in the depredation of Dutch Jews and the expropriation of their wealth. By German decree, all Dutch Jewish money, stocks, securities, and valuables were deposited in that bank. If K. V. Mulisch did not understand the true nature of this enterprise when he took the job, he certainly realized it as the months passed. Yet he remained in his post. And, with the connections he made, he protected his son, managed to get his former wife released after she had been picked up for deportation, and protected her too. She survived. Her relatives, the Jewish side of Harry's family, perished. For his role as a collaborator, K. V. Mulisch went to jail for three years.

Mulisch grew up to be one of four outstanding Dutch writers of his generation. All four had lived through the occupation and were shaped by it. As diverse as any four people could be, each had great talent and an enormous personality. Jan Wolkers's appetite for life translated into an interest in questions of the flesh. Willem Frederik Hermans, cynical and brilliant, had a fine eye for hypocrisy: if Wolkers was intimate, Hermans took a satirical, distant stance. Gerard van het Reve, wildly camp and wildly gay, celebrated a very public conversion to Roman Catholicism and explored his relationships with his boyfriends and the Virgin Mary. Mulisch, self-absorbed and famously vain, has pondered the big question of good and evil the whole of his extremely creative life. In a 2003 interview in the British newspaper, the *Guardian*, Mulisch remarked, "I am the second world war."* If that goes a bit far, it certainly is safe to say that Mulisch's family history illustrates moral choices, the absolutes of good and evil, and the ambiguity of each.

*David Horspool, "Mining the Past," *Guardian*, November 29, 2003.

Few in the Netherlands in 1961, including those who would read Mulisch's report, appreciated the ambiguities of their own wartime history. For them, the occupation was a black-and-white story of German suppression and Dutch resistance. The great mass of people who accommodated was left out. The Jews did not figure at all. No one thought about the issue of Dutch complicity in the genocide of the Jews. The first important scholarship about the war years, a four-volume work published between 1949 and 1954, bracketed the popular paradigm in its title: *Suppression and Resistance*. "The persecution of the Jews in the Netherlands, even if it happened on Dutch soil, is not properly Dutch history," one of the authors maintained. "It did not arise from Dutch circumstances. One can even say with certainty that it could not have arisen from it. The *resistance* against the persecution of the Jews has been a Dutch affair."*

The statue of the dockworker (1952) and the official Dutch memorial to the war years, the National Monument (1956) in Amsterdam, were merely official expressions of this interpretation of the war years. No public figure or statement acknowledged Dutch collaboration or that 80 percent of Holland's Jews had been murdered. Despite the films and photographs of the slave labor and death camps, the tangible aide-mémoire of returning Jews, as well as the intangible reminder of the memory of Jewish life in the Netherlands, the publication of Anne Frank's dairy in 1947 and the establishment of the foundation named after her in 1957, the fate of the Dutch Jews remained of marginal interest.

Eichmann's arrest and trial served as an early challenge to the Dutch national myth about the occupation period. If for most people the Holocaust was about specters in camps, his role highlighted the physical connection between the Netherlands and those camps. In an article in *Het Vrije Volk*, Johannes Buskes, an utterly fearless Protestant minister who had aided hidden Jews during the war (and who, precisely contrary to Pope Pius XII, had helped even those who had converted to return to

*Abel J. Herzberg, *Kroniek der Jodenvervolging, 1940–1945* (Amsterdam: Meulenhoff, 1985), p. 9.

Judaism after the war), raised uncomfortable questions about Dutch compliance and complicity. "We are not all mass murderers, but have not all of us soothed our conscience with very dubious arguments where the rescue of the Jews is concerned?"* Undaunted by his countrymen's violent response, Buskes went on to speak at a big public meeting held in Amsterdam the day after Eichmann's trial began in Jerusalem. The purpose of the forum was to address the fact that Eichmann had not worked alone. The Dutch people, Buskes declared, shared the responsibility for the persecution of the Dutch Jews.

This was a position Mulisch would adopt some five years later, but not in his reports on the trial in *Elseviers*. As he sat in the courtroom in Jerusalem, who Eichmann *was*—not what he *had done*—emerged as Mulisch's central concern. Eichmann, he observed, was "the calm, dutiful civil servant" (93). Hitler believed in his own revelations, "Himmler believed in Hitler, but Eichmann only believed in 'the order'" (93). Orders, Mulisch elaborated, carried a terrible, invincible bond for Eichmann, "something larger than the one giving it and the one receiving it—again as something mystical—as a superhuman power that has to be obeyed, no matter where it is coming from" (111). This explained, Mulisch argued, why Eichmann did not carry on murderous initiatives in Argentina: there was no order to do so. "Until Hitler's death Eichmann stood by his highest order. After that he became a 'peaceable citizen': that is, standing by the order of the society in which he *then* lived." This explained, too, why he behaved as he did when arrested by the Israelis. "He stood by the Israeli police and answered all the questions others would not have. [One of Eichmann's defense lawyers] told me that he would jump rope the whole day if they ordered him to jump rope the whole day" (112).

For Mulisch, this behavior or personality construct revealed something deeply horrifying about modern society. "He behaves

*Quoted in Ido de Haan, *Na de ondergang: De herinnering aan de Jodenvervolging in Nederland 1945–1955* (Den Haag: SDU, 1997), pp. 162 ff.

in Israel and Argentina for exactly the same reason that he behaved like an intimidating murderer in Europe: this is what was
expected of him. He *is* neither. He is nothing" (119). That nothingness defined Eichmann and marked the postwar world. "Figures such as Hitler and Himmler, the god and the believer, have
appeared before (though never with such a belief, celebrated on
such a scale); the 'Eichmann' appearance is a first" (109). Such
a man was "a machine that is good for anything." Worse: "Millions
like him are roaming the earth" (119).

Mulisch perceived Eichmann to be a tiny human being with
enormous technology at his disposal, a nothing, a machine. In the
wake of the atomic bomb and the arms race of the 1950s, such
people augured ill. "The danger that machines will change people
is not very great," Mulisch commented. "The danger is greater
that, together with these new machines, new, altered people will
appear too: people like machines, obeying their impulses, without
capability to examine their nature. That is why I called Eichmann
'the symbol of progress.'" This was not a trivial matter, Mulisch
warned. "It is dangerous to laugh off as excuses the invocations
of 'oath' and 'order,' which typify modern mechanical people like
Eichmann. To do so would be another attempt to fit them into a
reassuring psychology of the criminal mind, resulting in vigilance
falling asleep. We do not have to continue to be wary of criminals;
we must continue to be wary of perfectly ordinary people" (117).

Other reporters in the courtroom, most notably Hannah
Arendt, struggled with very much the same question: who was
Eichmann? What sort of man was he? By both training and biogra-
phy Arendt differed from Mulisch in significant respects. Born to
Jewish parents on October 14, 1906, in the Hanover of the kai-
ser's time, Arendt had enjoyed an extraordinary formal education
at the universities of Marburg and Heidelberg with intellectual lu-
minaries Martin Heidegger and Karl Jaspers. She became a political activist when Hitler came to power, and she landed in jail.
Released, she fled to Paris and was interned again, this time by
the French, when the Germans invaded. She escaped and made
her way to America in May 1941. Settling in New York, she became part of an intellectual Jewish community and an equally

intellectual, leftist, politically oriented, non-Jewish community. By the time of the Eichmann trial, Arendt had published her landmark *Origins of Totalitarianism* (1951) and *The Human Condition* (1958).

Perhaps because Arendt was a generation older and a generation more established than Mulisch, perhaps because she was a political philosopher and he a novelist, perhaps because she had been shaped by her experience of a German Jewish community with organized leadership during the prewar Nazi years and a vibrant Jewish community in America after the war while Mulisch knew none of that, she raised questions that simply did not occur to him. She argued, for example, that the Jewish councils bore some responsibility for the death of millions. She faulted them for insufficient perspicacity in recognizing the Nazis as a new breed of antisemites* who could not be bribed off or endured in silence. She accused the council members, too, of relishing power, of venality, and of selfishness. For myriad motives, they cooperated with Eichmann, and that cooperation amounted to collaboration. Nor did the victims escape her harsh judgment. She did not quite blame them for their own death, but nor did she shrink from holding them accountable for their failure to mount concerted political action.

If Mulisch did not share Arendt's focus on the role of the Jews in the machinery of death, he was as interested in the survivors and their court testimony as she. Eichmann, she pointed out, was on the stand for thirty-three and a half sessions. "Almost twice as many sessions, sixty-two . . . were spent on prosecution witnesses who, country after country, told their tales of horrors." She found

---

*The spelling "antisemites," which I use here, differs from the spelling in the body of the book. Introduced by Wilhelm Marr, a well-educated bigot and follower of Richard Wagner, the word "anti-Semite" proudly and consciously fused traditional anti-Judaism and modern racism. It is thus a racist word that has come into common parlance. I acknowledge the concept but wish to avoid exact repetition. Similarly, the word "exterminate," used by the Nazis to describe the murder of the Jews as vermin, has come into common parlance, too. Pests are exterminated. People are annihilated.

these sessions "endless." The witnesses could not tell a straight-forward story and entangled what had happened to them with what they "had read and heard and imagined." They simply did not have the "purity of soul . . . unmirrored, unreflected inno-cence of heart and mind that only the righteous possess" required to relate their life history with "shining honesty."* Mulisch, by contrast, saw the matter quite differently. He experienced the wit-nesses' testimony as a "blow" that hit him and everyone following the trial all over the world "hard." Their stories re-created the world they had endured two decades earlier. "Because the wit-nesses talked about past experiences, which will never truly be 'past' because they will always remain present to them, as if hap-pening today, and maybe even closer—that is why this 'today' cre-ated itself for those who did listen. The things they heard in the past few weeks happened only the moment the world heard them: in the spring of 1961" (87). This is the inverse of the question, If a tree falls in the forest and no one is there to hear it, has it really fallen? Only when the survivors spoke did actions take life and perpetrators take form. Mulisch borrowed the biblical image of creation—God said and there was—and used it to powerful effect: the survivors brought the Holocaust from the past into the pres-ent. Through their words it acquired reality, solidity.

Mulisch, unlike Arendt, did not analyze how relevant or re-dundant that testimony was. He did not worry about what was true memory and what, acquired knowledge. His worry, with regard to the testimony, centered around another matter entirely: the response of non-Jews. He noticed a certain "numbing," and in a fortnight "the opinion could be heard that the Jews had better stop talking about their misery; we knew already." But, Mulisch argued, "we will never know. It is not knowable. And resentment awakens in the listener who is confronted with the story that trivi-alizes the seriousness of his own [problems]" (87–88). Arendt's analysis is grounded in her academic training; Mulisch's in his insights as a novelist.

*Hannah Arendt, *Eichmann in Jerusalem* (New York: Penguin Books, 1994), pp. 223 ff.

For both Arendt the professor and Mulisch the high school dropout, however, the question of who Eichmann *was* sat at the core of the whole proceeding and their reports about it. Arendt adduced the thesis that the horror of Eichmann lay in the fact that he was nothing more than an ordinary man: a banal person for whom the organization of mass murder was an ordinary, banal, bureaucratic problem. For Mulisch, mass murder and the organization of mass murder were, by definition, most decidedly *not* banal. This was a contradiction in terms. Hardly ordinary or banal, Eichmann was the "machine man" shaped by the incredible power of new technology.

In the postscript for the revised and enlarged edition of her report a year after the original appeared in book form, Arendt noted three works published in the interim. One of these was Mulisch's, which she had read in German translation. His conclusions, she wrote, were "astonishingly similar to my own"; his "evaluation of Eichmann coincides with my own on some essential points."* Arendt erred. Their assessments and their analytic frameworks differed. Arendt, a social scientist, evaluated Eichmann by traditional, formal criteria: income, education, peer group, life expectations. And in all of these respects he was eminently ordinary. Mulisch, a novelist with a keen interest in the metaphysical, paid little attention to such factors. He saw Eichmann as the first "new man" and thus a herald of a dangerous development that can transform all of us into robots.

Arendt might have disagreed with Mulisch's identification of "the Eichmann appearance [as] a first" had she been willing to place the defendant in the context of the contemporary world, the world of 1961. She was not. Little influenced by events outside the window, Arendt sat in the Beit Ha'am (the House of the People) following the proceedings in the context of the courtroom with history and legal tradition in mind. Mulisch's context, by contrast, was the courtroom and the country. He analyzed the trial in its setting: the young state of Israel. His reports flow back and forth between the court and the city, the countryside, and even

*Ibid., pp. 281–82.

farther afield: Berlin, Warsaw, Auschwitz. If Mulisch perceived the trial as "the greatest public lesson in world history" (35), he perceived too that it was a building block in the growth of the new state. Israel had no long-established institutions; everything was new and untried. Mulisch appreciated the very fact that Israel existed and its exuberance and vitality: they framed the trial as an opportunity for creative nation-building. *Criminal Case 40/61* thus serves as a double report, with two sets of interconnected observations on the trial and on the development of the state.

We now know that trials are not public lessons in world history. Trials are trials, and history is history. Nor did this trial accomplish what Mulisch hoped: bury the Nazi era for good (23). On the contrary, there have been a number of trials since the Eichmann case, and the number of books, articles, films, and artworks about the Nazi era grows each year. The Nazi years are the only historical period in the modern age to generate ever greater interest in subsequent decades. Most particularly, the enormity and significance of the Holocaust emerge more clearly as time passes, rather than fade away.

From our vantage point in 2005, we can situate the Eichmann trial in history, and we can analyze Eichmann with the help of the historical research of the past forty-five years. And while the Eichmann case was not a history lesson, it was a pivotal event: it reframed the historical significance of the Holocaust and it exploded a public silence barrier. That silence barrier, erected by the Germans during the Holocaust, remained strong in the postwar period. The signal importance of the Holocaust simply was not acknowledged: Europeans had other (and to them, more pressing) concerns. The establishment of Israel in 1948 had not broken the barrier either; silence reigned in Israel too. Little sympathy was expended on the "victims." Rather, the "martyrs and heroes" of the Jewish resistance were acknowledged and valorized. Yom ha-Shoah (Holocaust Remembrance Day), established by the Israeli parliament in 1951, was linked on the calendar to the Warsaw Ghetto uprising. After all, the new Israeli government had other (and to them, more pressing) concerns: hostile neighboring states, a weak economy, a country that wanted for nearly everything, and hundreds of thousands of traumatized fresh immigrants. They wanted survivors to become strong and to join the infant state in its mission. The government's goal was not to deal with the problems the survivors had brought with them, but to reform and refashion them into future citizens.

The survivors understood. They learned Hebrew and abandoned the language, culture, and traditions of the world of their birth. They did not speak in public about what had happened to them in Europe. But it is not true that survivors of the Holocaust fell silent. What is true is that, as there was no public forum for their voice, they spoke to each other and at *Landsmanschaften* ([European] hometown fraternal organization) meetings. There were islands of speech, of articulated memory, but these islands were not in the public sphere.

Eichmann's trial broke the taboo. The Holocaust—the murder of the European Jews—was the central issue before a court for the first time. And the highly visible witnesses for the prosecution were Jews. For the first time, survivors were prominent, present, and publicly vocal. They could not testify about Eichmann's role or German criminal responsibility. But they—and only they—could describe how their daily lives had been shaped by the criminals and their crimes. Their experiences in the German-decreed ghettos, hunted by the *Einsatzgruppen*, in the camps were essential to the court proceedings. The voices of the survivors and the suffering of the victims were acknowledged, honored, and legitimized.

We now know, as Mulisch and Arendt could not have at the time, how important this was for research and teaching about the Holocaust in the years that followed. And that research, in turn, has opened new interpretations of Eichmann. The immediate interest in the psychological motivation of the bureaucratic murderer prompted by the trial ultimately was reshaped by survivors' accounts of what had happened to them. Investigating precisely *how* rather than *why* Eichmann accomplished the bureaucratic system that had brought millions to their death, another Eichmann emerged. From our study of the Holocaust, my coauthor Robert Jan van Pelt and I would describe Eichmann as anything but ordinary and certainly not a machine man. Analyzing the structures he created, we see Eichmann as enormously inventive and creative. He approached each situation anew and responded in a flexible fashion to achieve his deadly goals. And he was ambitious, overweeningly ambitious. Mulisch understood something of that at the very end of his report. Writing on September 23, 1961, Mulisch pondered the Pavlovian admixture of killing and success for Eichmann. "So what must the murder of the Jews mean for Eichmann? Linked up with the power, the status, the uniform, the car with chauffeur, the mistresses, the *Schnaps*, the parties, and of course the beautiful things he saw: the cities, Budapest, the music he heard, his children—but *naturally* tears come to his eyes, with emotion and nostalgia when thinking back to the days of the gas chambers. How could anyone assume that he would show fear or remorse when hearing the witnesses: those were the good old days" (160).

A Few Suggestions for Further Reading

Little has appeared in English on the early postwar response (1945 until the Eichmann trial in 1961) to the Holocaust in the Netherlands, or on Harry Mulisch. The following therefore includes a few of the major relevant Dutch works.

Aschheim, Steven E., ed. *Hannah Arendt in Jerusalem*. Berkeley and Los Angeles: University of California Press, 2001.

Buurlage, Jos. *Onveranderlijk veranderlijk: Harry Mulisch tussen literatuur, journalistiek en politiek in de jaren zestig en zeventig*. Amsterdam: De Bezige Bij, 1999.

Council of Jews from Germany. *In the Wake of the Eichmann Trial*. London: Waldon Press, 1964.

Donner, J. H. *Mulisch, naar ik veronderstel*. Amsterdam: De Bezige Bij, 1971.

Dwork, Debórah and van Pelt, Robert Jan. *Holocaust: A History.* New York: W. W. Norton, 2002.

Dwork, Debórah and van Pelt, Robert Jan. "The Netherlands." In David S. Wyman, ed., *The World Reacts to the Holocaust.* Baltimore: Johns Hopkins University Press, 1996, pp. 45–77.

Hondius, Dienke. *Return: Holocaust Survivors and Dutch Anti-Semitism.* Trans. David Colmer. Westport, Conn.: Praeger, 2003.

Sannes, H. W. J. *Onze Juden en Duitschland's Greep naar de Wereldmacht.* Amsterdam: Uitgeversmaatschppij te Amsterdam, 1946.

Yablonka, Hanna. *The State of Israel vs. Adolf Eichmann.* Trans. Ora Cummings with David Herman. New York: Schocken Books, 2004.

1

Introduction

"40/61" is the number of the Eichmann case on the roll of the District Court of Jerusalem. In this volume, I give the account of an experience behind this number. An experience is different from a train of thought: it is subject to change. At the end one finds a different person, partly with different thoughts, from at the beginning. Since the account of this changing experience is announced in the first entry, I have not made any corrections anywhere: this was not supposed to be a book about Eichmann, but to remain the double report as it was intended from the start.

What follows are not the chapters of a dissertation but a series of articles originally published in *Elseviers Weekblad* (a weekly, so that I was relieved of the dailies' demands of providing the news). For that reason I dated them with the day of completion, not of publication, which was usually one week later. This will avoid confusion with the dates of the diary sections. I did rid the text of some inaccuracies, mainly in the diary. I have added a short passage here and there, which would not have been suitable for a weekly. Where possible quotations are in German, for in Dutch* they are no longer what they are: dangerous. For those who cannot read German, one of the most important entrances to criminal case 40/61 will in this way remain closed—maybe that makes them fortunate.

*For this English translation the quotations are given in English, so that this important entrance to criminal case 40/61 will be accessible. (All footnotes are the translator's unless otherwise indicated.)

1

2

$\boxed{3/26/61}$

The Verdict and the Execution

Mankind has forever known the scene of a lone individual, facing his own destruction, as embodied by a tribunal of men representing society. In some way or other, we humans all doubt our own deaths, that is to say: we doubt reality. In *the trial* we will be confronted most mercilessly with its existence.

Sometimes such a trial is unforgettable because of its symbolic meaning, and our sympathy lies wholly on the side of the accused. Such is the case in the trial of Socrates, in fifth-century B.C. Athens. Sometimes such a trial changes the face of mankind, as in the trial of Jesus, in Jerusalem, around 30 A.D. Since the conviction of the innocent lay embedded in the task "to fulfill the Scripture," the possible attitudes toward these cases are no longer of an inter-human nature. Sometimes such a trial is remembered because it was pitiful and dirty, as is the case with the trial of Joan of Arc, in Rouen, 1431. Sometimes such a trial marks immense political changes, as was the case with the trial of Louis XVI, in Paris, 1793. As for the latter, one can argue on which side sympathy should lie. But never in world history has mankind, so unanimously lacking sympathy, been so prepared to destroy one man as in the case of Adolf Eichmann, in Jerusalem, 1961.

So why are the Nuremberg trials not among these trials? After all, there people who were even more directly guilty, or guilty to a higher degree, than Eichmann were made to stand trial. One might say that in 1946 nobody wanted to hear about the war; the scum had to be hanged as quickly as possible, and that would be the end of it. Certain facts were too unbelievable at the time, such as the horrible eyewitness account by SS officer Kurt Gerstein concerning the gas chambers (he had passed this information on to Sweden and the Vatican in 1942; to no avail, by the way). On the other hand, by now, in 1961, the war has turned modern: war novels are best sellers, documentaries fill movie theaters all over the world. There is a new generation wanting to know everything, with all sorts of nice and dubious motives. Yet the overwhelming interest in the Eichmann trial cannot simply be attributed to the distance we have gained from the war. Without a doubt, the most important reason lies in the fact that in Jerusalem, one man appears before his judges, whereas in Nuremberg it was a group of twenty. That was group versus group, which is different from all against one.

All against one—that is a trial: that is reality. The innocent, Socrates and Jesus, did not need a trial to wake up to reality: they were more real than their judges: they died as the judges of their judges. The bloodied soldier Joan of Arc lost herself exaltedly in her "voices," which had changed into the flames of the stake. The decapitated Louis Capet is too insignificant a person to be looked into; this was made unnecessary anyway, by the revealing words of Danton: "We do not want to condemn the king, we want to kill him." But he who stands trial for murder, or for a million murders, committed the crime because he embodied his own reality, because he doubted reality. He is taught a lesson by means of a trial, in which reality shows itself by striking back. (In this case, reality is shaped by the same Jews for whom he himself was once the monstrous reality.)

Not only did Eichmann not know what he was doing when he transported his victims by the hundred of thousands to the gas chambers; in a sense he did not even know *that* he was doing something. I don't mean "legal accountability" or anything like that—those are tiny concepts by tiny judges for tiny bastards. No, if you did what Eichmann did, you are not so different from us, but even more wickedly alienated from life on Earth—and especially from death on Earth. The Chinese punished the Hwang Ho when it exceeded its banks and killed thousands of people. The difference between the Hwang Ho and Eichmann lies in our declaring him guilty in a trial. It would no doubt be a reassurance to mankind if the accused were consumed by remorse. But he said that he would jump into his grave laughing, in the knowledge that he was responsible for the death of five million Jews. They asked him whether he felt remorse. He said: "Remorse is for children." Of course, one can only respond indignantly to this kind of comment; one can also try to use it as a key to one of the many locks that keep this man hermetically hidden. Then one has to come to the conclusion that this is a wickedly unreal person, alienated from himself. Maybe the remorse of a human being is inadequate to encompass the destruction of millions. No doubt, if he had claimed to be remorseful, that would have satisfied the weak-kneed part of mankind; but for the dead and for the survivors it would have been more insulting. His deeds are beyond remorse, contrition, or a guilty conscience; they are out of any proportion to any word or concept. This eclipsed person can only become guilty by a verdict. At the same time this may set his halted soul in motion again. It may come as a liberation for him. When he was arrested in Buenos Aires on May 11, 1960, he showed signs of relief.

In this respect, he is better off than the pilots of the *Enola Gay*, who dropped the atomic bomb on Hiroshima. Upon their return, they were given a hero's welcome. One pilot immediately entered a monastery. The other, Claude Eatherly, has had regular brushes with the law for all sorts of minor offenses such as shoplifting. Every time some psychiatrist has explained that this man only stole, of course, because he was seeking punishment. After all, he was the Hiroshima man. Then the case would be dismissed, and the public punishment he was longing for would elude him again. In 1959 he was admitted to an insane asylum. The last report is that he escaped that too—naturally because it did not involve any punishment.* If the United States really wants to do something for its great son, it should give him life in prison.

Eichmann is lucky that he was not on the winning, but the losing side. He is not a war hero, but a war criminal. He can be found guilty. In his trial, his deeds will be hooked up with reality, that is, with his death. A greater service cannot be rendered to him. He understood this when his captors gave him the choice in Argentina: either you come to Israel for a trial, or you will be executed on the spot. On the other hand, the feeling of dissatisfaction expressed in many living rooms that he can only die one death, and not six million, is unnecessary. Calculations including death cannot be made. Six million times zero still equals zero. This death sentence will be a just verdict. It does not even have to be accelerated by an execution.

The verdict is for Eichmann; his execution is intended for us. We will be left with the feeling that something has been done. That something *can* be done. That justice can be done. But man cannot do justice. He can only kill: even when it is done in the form of an "execution" following a death sentence. Justice can only be *administered*. The judge and the hangman are two distinct people. A judge who executes his own sentences would be an unspeakably barbaric institution. When word came of Eichmann's arrest last year, countless people offered to kill him; but when it became known that he was to be sentenced at a trial, and therefore that the killing would be done not by a judge but by a hangman, the Israeli authorities had a hard time finding someone for the job.

The judge knows what he is saying. But the hangman who may hang Eichmann is someone just like him: he does not know what he is doing, because that deed *cannot* be known. Death withdraws from us in all forms, except for our own death,—that is why the Greek poisoned cup, the forced suicide, is perhaps the most transparent form of a death sentence. So with this realization we must let the hangman do his dirty work later (*if* he gets to do it):

*On June 12, 1961, Major Eatherly was recaptured; in August he escaped again.—Author.

with the realization that it is not for Eichmann, and not for his victims, but for us, the survivors.

It is one of the most fantastic twists of history that this trial will be held in Jerusalem, in the same city where a man about whom it is said, mysteriously, that "he has taken on the sins of mankind" was convicted. Now a man who allegedly has really almost committed those sins is standing trial. It is impossible to relate to it on a human basis. Indeed, an unmistakably half-religious tone resounds in the myriad of books and articles already published about the Eichmann trial. Evil pinpointed! The bad in the guise of a human being: the Devil Eichmann! But we cannot begin to *believe* in Eichmann. Whatever hidden form they take, and no matter how well intended, such reassuring fantasies of an Anti-Christ are a delusion that we cannot allow anyone to accept.

Of the crimes committed under Hitler's power reach, the neo-Nazis (not Eichmann) say: all lies. The Germans say: it was the Nazis who committed them. The Europeans say: it was the Germans. The Americans say: it was the Europeans. The Asians and Africans say: it was the whites. And at some point people will say: it was people. But never may we say: it was Eichmann.

In two weeks' time we will go to Jerusalem, from all parts of the world—like medieval lepers, having heard about a new source that cures all diseases. There we will write the page of history about which the chief of the German police, Heinrich Himmler, said to high-ranking SS officers, on October 4, 1943: "Most of you know what it means when 100 bodies lie together, when 500 lie there, or if 1,000 lie there. To have gone through this and at the same time, apart from exceptions caused by human weakness, to have remained decent, that has made us hard. This is a chapter of glory in our history which has never been written, and which never shall be written."*

We will write it, probably producing a corpse in the process . . . and return home still lepers. Most importantly, I will report about *this* trial, about us, about ourselves, those reading this.

*Secret meeting of SS officers in Poznan, Poland, In *Document No. 1919-PS*, Nuremberg trial, translated by Carlos Porter.

3

The Two Faces of Eichmann

Before looking into Eichmann's life before 1938, the year he was sent to Vienna, or into his adventures after 1945 (the seven years in between will come to light in Jerusalem), we have time to study his face. A little trick may help us do that.

Figure 1 is a photograph of Eichmann, taken on June 8, 1960, shortly after his abduction to Israel. Figures 2 and 3 are portraits of men who have never existed and who never will. They were created by halving Eichmann's photo straight down the middle and completing it with its mirror image.

The first impulse is: *that* is the real Eichmann, figure 3: the barbaric, twisted mug of the mass murderer. Figure 2, on the other hand, is very human: a calm face, serious eyes, and a glimmer of a smile around his mouth. But doubt creeps in when studying the two pictures a little longer, doubt about this simple interpretation. For this reason, some technical corrections must be considered.

The light in Eichmann's photo comes from the upper left and from behind on the right. As a result, the shadowy parts on the right side of his face are doubled in figure 3, in which the light seems to be coming mainly from behind and upwards, with a sinister result. The background is totally dark here. For analogous reasons, figure 2 seems to be bathed in sunlight against a lit background.

9

Figure 1

Figure 3 shows a significantly smaller head than figure 2, which draws attention to the sagging, dislocated right half of Eichmann's head. Last year, when he was kidnapped on the streets of Buenos Aires by Israeli agents, they took him to a house outside the city. There they undressed him and first checked for the SS

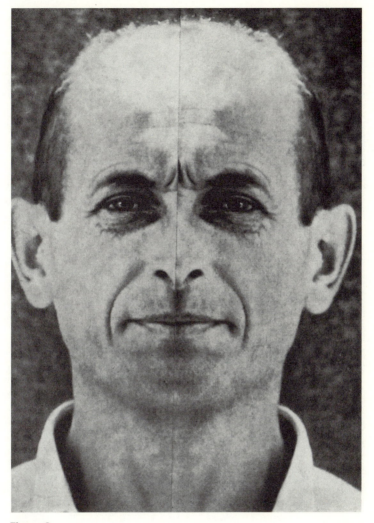

Figure 2

symbols under his left armpit (there was a scar: he had tried to remove the tattoo himself with a knife). Second, they put an SS hat on him and compared him to a photograph, and third, using old X-rays, they found a fracture in his collar bone and in his skull (after this they finally spoke to him, saying: "You are Adolf Eich-

11

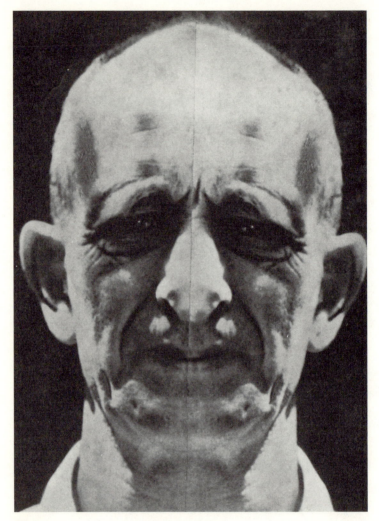

Figure 3

mann"). I suppose that it is this old fracture in his skull that makes the head in figure 3 so small. The protruding right ear returns with its ugly double. The mouth, distorted to the right, and the sagging right eye—everything appears mercilessly.

But now this: who looks more like Eichmann, 2 or 3? There

Figure 4

can be no doubt: figure 2. This does undermine the theory that 2 is the human and 3 the beast. Do modern murderers really have such frighteningly distorted faces? Then I remembered something. In 1956 I visited concentration camp Buchenwald near Weimar. The barracks, infected with typhoid, had been burned shortly after the war, but the main buildings were still there: the gate with its iron rail, in which the words JEDEM DAS SEINE [TO EACH HIS OWN] were elegantly welded; the cells; the building with the shot-in-the-back-of-the-neck installation (a room, painted red, in which one was "measured": as soon as the top strip was placed over the head, a pistol was aimed through a crack in the wall, exactly at the neck, while loudspeakers played cheerful music across the camp to drown out the sound of the shots); the concrete cellars with dozens of hooks around on the walls, on which the prisoners were to hang each other; the floor, which, just like in bathrooms, was laid with an edge up along the walls: for the

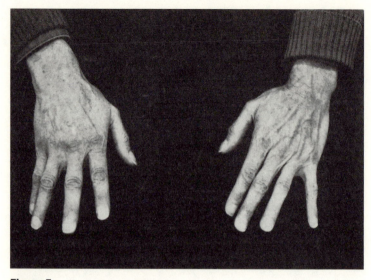

Figure 5

blood; an iron elevator which led straight to the crematorium. The man who showed me around did not accompany me into the cellar. Although he had been an attendant in this camp for eleven years, he waited outside. He was the spitting image of figure 3, except his nose was smashed in addition. He was not an ex-camp bully, but one of the oldest prisoners: at the start of Buchenwald in 1938 he was brought in as a Communist. He had been through everything.

That is why I believe we will be getting closer to the truth if we see the *witness* in figure 3. Figure 3 is the face that sees what the man in figure 2 does. Figure 2 is the slick, unmoved, merciless face of the killer; figure 3 is the face that observes the killing, filled with horror. Or: if figure 2 is Eichmann, then figure 3 is the face of the world watching him at work. Returning to Eichmann's real face: the right-hand side is the part on which his crimes have had an effect, the side of the heart; the left-hand side is the part that committed the crimes.

Had figure 2 been Eichmann's face, then they could have shot him in Argentina, without any trial. But now that there is that

14

other side of his face, embodied by the tormented horror of figure 3, I for one would not even throw the one-thousandth stone very quickly. This is the enigmatic face of the man who, in 1939, gave the order to punish severely anyone who desecrated Theodor Herzl's grave in Vienna. Herzl was the founder of Zionism. At the thirty-fifth commemoration of his death, perplexed Jews saw a lone figure in civilian clothes at the tomb. It was Eichmann.

4

4/2/61

Biography of a German

1906–1938: A CAREER. NSDAP #889895 and SS #45326 was born in Solingen on March 19, 1906. This city in the Rhineland is known for its knife industry, which developed from its medieval sword forging. His mother died when he was nine, and his father decided to emigrate to Linz, Austria. Together with his three brothers and one sister, Adolf (i.e., Eichmann, for Hitler, too, spent his youth in this city) was raised by an aunt. He is said to have had no friends, preferring solitary reading. This is supposed to help explain the mass murder. But it is also said that he was the leader of a youth gang that beat up Jewish boys. This, too, is supposed to explain the mass murder. He allegedly kept exact tallies of the beatings, one of which is said to have led to a suicide. All kinds of things are being said now. What seems to be certain is that he was often called "Jew," due to his dark complexion and his big nose.

After four years he left the Staatsoberrealschule without a diploma, and for two years he was enrolled in the Höhere Bundeslehranstalt für Verkehrstechnik, Maschinenbau und Hochbau. In one version (in which his father is poor and a failure) he leaves this school for lack of money; in the other version (which makes his father a wealthy man) he leaves for lack of interest and restlessness.

17

In 1925 he got a job with the Oberösterreichischer Elektro-bau A.G., and two years later, at age twenty-one, he became a representative (and peddler) with the American Vacuum Oil Company in Vienna. Then he traveled across Austria on a heavy, red motorcycle. It was a happy time for him. He learned to drink and to have sex, two things that kept him busy for the rest of his life. In 1932 he had a serious traffic accident, in which he broke his left hand and fractured his skull in two places. The deformed hand later prevented him from obtaining sports awards, which Himmler had made obligatory for all SS men [see figure 5]. The X-rays of the skull fractures helped to identify him in Argentina in 1960. Some have suggested that the fractures resulted in brain damage: this should help explain the mass murder. I do not believe the court in Jerusalem will be inclined to accept the reduction of the death of hundreds of thousands to lonely reading, youth gang membership, or riding drunk on a red motorbike.

In addition to women and booze, Eichmann got to know two kinds of people during this period: Jews and Nazis. The Jews of Vienna, who represented to a large extent the culture of their city, must have touched something incomprehensible in him. It appears that he interacted with them regularly, visiting their bookstores and eateries, even picking up a few words of Yiddish and Hebrew, and he must have been to a synagogue then too. What Oriental dream did he recognize here? One that would connect his name forever to Jewry? What Oriental dream of civilization, religion, pathos, resignation, and solidarity? I know I am being vague and mysterious—but speaking more clearly here would be more deceitful. Nothing indicates that he simply hated the Jews. Murder does not necessarily point to hatred. Maybe he *wanted* to hate them; maybe he hated them because he loved them. Maybe this is a mechanism that leads more strongly to murder. In any case, it is a more complicated mechanism than that of Hitler or Himmler, who hated the Jews much more simply, albeit based on greater ignorance (is hatred, especially anti-Semitism, ever simple?). More than ten years after the war, Eichmann told a friend (the Dutch SS man Wim Sassen, who sold his notes to *Life* in 1960): "I no longer remember exactly when, but it was even before Rome itself had been founded that the Jews could already write. It is very depressing for me to think of that people writing laws over 6,000 years of written history. But it tells me that they must be a people of the first magnitude, for lawgivers have always been great."*

One can stare at such expressions for a long time. This is the man who was treated by the Jews of Vienna as one of their own thirty years ago, for they, too, recognized his nose—the man who sent them to their deaths soon after—the man who in Israel is now awaiting the enforcement of a Jewish law that was designed especially for him, six thousand years later.

Will we get one step, one tiny step, closer to the truth by saying that he *wanted* something like this? Not exactly this, but something like this: a blood wedding with Jewry, which in any case meant his own extermination, a piece of disgusting excrement—I beg your pardon, but I can only speak in images. What made Eichmann tick was at most an image, not an idea. Even at that, an image that will remain in the darkness forever because it *is* darkness.

But no matter what dream or image turned inside out is responsible for it: he joined the Nationalsozialistische Deutsche Arbeiterpartei [NSDAP], the Austrian chapter, on April 1, 1932. Perhaps he occasionally went by bike to Berchtesgaden, just across the border, where Hitler lived and where he held meetings.

From then on, his whole life changed. He was fired by the Vacuum Oil Company, joined the more or less illegal Austrian SS, took an oath of loyalty to the führer before Himmler, and was given orders to go to Germany in early 1933. He received military training and for eight months was part of the SS contingency in the recently established concentration camp at Dachau, for Hitler had meanwhile ascended to power. On October 1, 1934, *SS*-Unterscharführer Eichmann was transferred to the SD-Hauptamt in Munich, which moved to Berlin shortly thereafter.

Increasingly, a rivalry within the Nazi party developed be-

*Adolf Eichmann, "To Sum It All Up, I Regret Nothing," *Life* December 5, 1960, p. 161.

tween the SA and the SS. The Sturmabteilung, led by the old war-horse Ernst Röhm, wore brown uniforms and consisted of a savage gang of incredible bastards. The Schutzstaffel also consisted of incredible bastards, but in black uniforms. They were smaller in number, and via Himmler they were under the direct command of Hitler himself. Originally they were his personal life-guards, and they were earmarked for the future aristocracy of the Thousand-Year Reich. Himmler founded the Sicherheitsdienst in 1931, as a division of the disciplined, semi-mystical order of the SS. Their commander was Reinhard Heydrich, a twenty-seven-year-old naval officer, discharged because he refused to marry a girl who was pregnant by him (his reasoning: she was no longer a virgin). This sinister, still underestimated individual was probably the biggest genius of all the Nazis, including Himmler and Hitler, who were both under his influence. Heydrich detached the SD from the SS, although it was intended as the party's equivalent of the army's intelligence, the Abwehr, and built it into a mechanism that kept especially close tabs on the party itself. Thanks to these "brains" of the party, Hitler could soon rid himself of his rivals. On June 30, 1934 (the "Night of the Long Knives"), he had Röhm killed because he had become useless, and for weeks on end Himmler's SS killed thousands of Hitler's opponents within and outside the party, led by the all-seeing eye of the SD. Then the SA was done for, and the road to almost absolute power lay open for Himmler and Heydrich.

A few months after these events, Eichmann came to work at the SD, as a clerk in cataloging. It is here that he discovered one day that Hitler's cook, who was also his mistress for a while, was one thirty-second Jewish. His superiors, shocked to death, immediately locked this report away, classified as top secret. But in general Eichmann was obedient, diligent, and punctual. Shortly thereafter he requested permission to marry Vera Liebl, a Sudeten German blonde. (Recently she sent him a dark suit from Argentina, so that he will look neat during his trial.) The SS headquarters examined her genealogy, checked the three pictures in a bathing suit, and a medical certificate, and they graciously gave permission for the marriage. Not long thereafter Klaus Eichmann was born. (After his father's transfer to Israel he wrote: "I cannot believe what they are saying about you. The tree you planted is growing well, and I water it regularly.") The happy father was promoted to *Hauptscharführer* and transferred to division II-112, Judentum (Jewry).

It was 1936 now. Himmler had succeeded in uniting the entire police organization under his command, into a Hauptamt Sicherheitspolizei; the Geheime Staatspolizei (Gestapo) was part of it. With Heydrich as the actual creator in the background, he now ruled the most powerful terror organization in world history, which he continually had Heydrich adapt to changing circumstances.

In 1937 Eichmann submitted a request to be allowed to continue his Hebrew studies, under a rabbi; cost: 3 marks per hour. A worried Heydrich refused: would a Jew be able to teach a National Socialist anything? So Eichmann continued diligently, on his own, to develop into a specialist on Jewish affairs. He set up a "Jewish museum" for the SD, read everything possible about Jewry, and gathered data about Zionist activities in the British mandate Palestine.

He was sent there with a colleague in September 1937, in order to coordinate the anti-Jewish activities of the Arabs—that is one version. The other: to negotiate all sorts of more or less obscure matters with the Hagannah, the illegal organization of Jewish fighters, whose anti-British politics were on a par with those of the Germans. The report proposing him for the mission said Eichmann was reliable, educated, an expert in his field, very precise, ambitious, presentable in appearance, self-assured, easy to get along with, with organizational skills and an impeccable personal attitude toward life; he was also a confirmed National Socialist.

The two German "journalists" had barely set foot on Palestinian soil when the intelligence service knew who they were. Forty-eight hours later they were back on the boat. More than twenty years later Eichmann certified in Argentina (before his arrest): "I did see enough to be very impressed by what the Jewish colonists were building up their land. I admired their desperate will to live,

the more so since I myself was an idealist. In the years that followed I often said to Jews with whom I had dealings that, had I
been a Jew, I would have been a fanatical Zionist. I could not
imagine being anything else. In fact, I would have been the most
ardent Zionist imaginable."*

The frightening part is that he means it. One cannot imagine
Hitler, Himmler, or Heydrich saying such things. Eichmann hated
every Jew who was not Jewish enough to go to Palestine. Did he
think the Jews were *inadequate* as Jews? Had he imagined them
as some sort of gods—and they turned out to be only human? Did
he, following this inhumane demand, become inhumane himself?
And should one surmise that he, as "the most ardent Zionist imaginable," would have been willing to gas the Arabs by the millions?

There are no answers. What we see is that even in Argentina
he identified with the Jews. During the war he went so far in this
that he spread the rumor that he had been born in Palestine—not
as a Jew, of course, but as a German Templar, but this is irrelevant
here. He is said to have visited a concentration camp once to have
a number of Jews called up. He asked who spoke Hebrew. Of
course nobody answered: who knows, maybe it meant death. He
then lost himself in a scolding, saying that these Jews did not
speak Hebrew, but he, an SS officer, spoke Hebrew! (This was
hardly true, by the way.)

Back in Germany he was promoted to *Untersturmführer*. A
little later, the Austrian secretary Dr. Arthur Seyss-Inquart handed
his country to Hitler, and the same day Eichmann was sent to
Vienna, where he announced his first measures against his former
friends, only a few hours after his arrival. It was 1938. Now the
time period began, which he described in Argentina: "I was not
asleep during the war years."†

1938–1945: BUT WAS HE AWAKE? It remains to be seen whether
in Jerusalem, at least in the courtroom, much will be said about

---

*Adolf Eichmann, "I Transported Them . . . to the Butcher," *Life*,
November 28, 1960, p. 22.
†Ibid., p. 21.

what happened to him in the following seven years. They will determine what he did, and how much of that can legally be held against him.

Rudolf Höss, camp commander of Auschwitz, testified in Nuremberg that already in 1943 Eichmann no longer believed in a German victory. But the crime that will probably be counted most heavily against him, the deportation of over 400,000 Hungarian Jews, did not take place until one year later. "If Germany collapses," he once said to his close subordinate and friend, Dieter von Wisliceny, "at least we will be able to say that we have achieved something. We will have completely exterminated the European Jews." Three months before the end of the war, he said to his SS baron that he would commit suicide should Germany capitulate.

But the *Hauptsturmführer* knew his friend inside and out. Eichmann was too scared ever to use a plane. He was always afraid of attempts on his life; he never traveled without hand grenades and machine guns in his car. He had even had the foresight never to allow people to take pictures of him. Those who did had to hand over the roll of film. In a Czech cell, awaiting his execution for war crimes (1946; thirty-four years old), Wisliceny signed a statement in which he decidedly said he was convinced that Eichmann was alive and hiding in Austria, and that he would be able to find him within weeks.

Had they accepted his offer, Eichmann would probably have been dead for many years now. I am not sad that this did not happen. It would have been an Eichmann with a right side of the face that had not been devastated by the signs his past has engraved on it during fifteen years of remembering. And the world would have missed the trial, with which the Nazi era will now be buried for good.

1945–1960: ADOLF BARTH, ADOLF ECKMANN, OTTO HENINGER, RICARDO KLEMENT. At the end of April 1945, the thirty-nine-year-old Eichmann made his way south, through a disintegrating Germany, slipped through the pincers of Konyev's and Eisenhower's armies, and reached Austria, which he had left twelve years earlier as a fired traveling gas salesman. In Alt Aussee he ran into all sorts of fleeing Nazi dogs, among whom was Ernst Kaltenbrunner, his boss since 1942 when Heydrich was killed. But this optimist thought Eichmann's company was too dangerous, and he ordered him to disappear. The *SS-Obersturmbannführer* decided to "become" a corporal with the Luftwaffe. He visited his family one last time, gave his Vera four poison capsules in case the Russians got there first, and walked away westward, to stay out of Soviet hands at least.

It did not take long before an American patrol picked him up. They interned him as Adolf Barth, one of two million prisoners of war. When his SS membership tattoo was discovered some time later, he said that he was an officer of the Waffen SS, and that he had nothing to do with the political SS, and that his real name was Adolf Eckmann. As place of birth he gave Breslau: he knew that the birth register there had been destroyed.

In the course of 1945 he moved from one internment camp to the next—until the fear of discovery became too intense for him. Repeatedly his name came up at the Nuremberg tribunal, and in January 1946 his deputy, Wisliceny, gave a very detailed account of his activities. Eichmann's interrogators began to doubt his words too; furthermore, he suspected (and rightly so) that there were Jews already on the lookout for him: those were the ones he feared most. The underground SS committee in the camp gave him permission to flee and supplied him with some addresses. Provided with false identification papers, he left.

Lumberjack Otto Heninger, who lived on the Lüneberg Heath for four years, was a neat, taciturn man, who often spent hours walking through the woods. One day, unexpectedly, he was gone.

The international neo-Nazi central organization ODESSA (Organisation der SS-Angehörigen) supplied Arab countries with stolen weapons and ammunition in exchange for marijuana and opium. The profits from the sale of these drugs were used to smuggle war criminals out of the country. In the spring of 1950, Eichmann arrived in Rome—without hindrance, since the British and American security services were almost exclusively interested in Communist organizations. He is said to have traveled as a monk.

In any case, he was lodged in a monastery, also later in Genoa. Maybe they took him for a refugee from behind the Iron Curtain, and maybe not. It does not explain, in any case, why he had to be smuggled so secretly through a free Italy, from monastery to monastery. However it may be, in June the Vatican gave him a refugee pass in the name of Ricardo Klement. A few days later he had his Argentinean visa, and in July he entered the country of Juan Perón.

Continuously protected and supported by the powerful Nazi underground, Eichmann got a job with a contractor on the Chilean border, and in 1952 he received money to have his family reunited with him, something that happened unnoticed due to the inattentiveness of the Jewish agents. When Perón had to flee, the movement lost some of its power. Eichmann worked at a rabbit farm, set up a small laundromat, lost it due to Chinese competition, and finally got a job as a mechanic in a Mercedes-Benz plant. He procreated once more: Ricardo Liebl was born. Eichmann no longer existed, and Klement and Vera lived as common-law man and wife. That is what his life was like then. He lived in a house that was much like a gas chamber. Right before the Jews came, he said: "I would like to find peace with my former opponents."*

1960: A HUNTING SCENE. The first pictures that man drew in the dark caves show frail, tumbling figures that are spraying a gigantic beast with arrows. But sometimes there is a third figure, in addition to the beast and the hunter. Sometimes there is a shape behind the hunter, with his arms raised. Between them a line is drawn—that is power flowing to the first from the second, who is the wizard, or the god, or the dead . . .

The three hunters that were finally standing before him were named Yigal, Gad, and Dov—mysterious Oriental sounds, just like he must have heard them in Vienna for the first time, thirty-five years ago. "I have always known that it would go like this," he said, when he was naked and shivering on a chair facing them: a thin, aged body, of which he was ashamed.

*Eichmann, "To Sum It All Up, I Regret Nothing," p. 161.

5

$$4/6-29/61$$

Jerusalem Diary I

Thursday, April 6. Maybe a crusader, dying of thirst, once had a vision of such a trip to Jerusalem: flying over the snow covered Alps, over Florence, Rome, Naples, along the Greek islands, across Crete, to the Holy Land. Invited into the cockpit, I am overcome by a sense of safety and alienation. It is dawning on me that the plane is not moving. With thousands of buttons and gauges, the four men control the slow movement of the Earth underneath us. Over Tel Aviv bags of dark clouds have been emptied, shot through with lightning.

The alienation is complete when I am at the airport. My first time outside Europe! A friendly gentleman from the embassy is waiting for me, and a little later we are floating into the hills in an American car on the same road that the Romans once marched, and the crusaders trudged a thousand years later. In vain I try to make out some of the landscape. It is starting to rain. All of a sudden we have to stop: there is a man lying in the light of our spotlights, in the middle of the road, trying to get up. But it turns out to be a porcupine, slowly shuffling into the road's dark shoulder. It is dark everywhere. When I am told that we are passing an Arab village, Abu Ghosh, I start to have doubts. After an hour of driving, we are entering a deserted city of yellow stone. It is raining. We are leaving the city again. I do not believe we were in a city. Fifteen minutes later I am dropped off at a dripping hostel. As I watch the car disappear, I am regretting my plans. Everybody is asleep. A grumpy old man puts on a raincoat over his pajamas and takes me through the yard to a small annex. In the dark I can make out a palm tree, but I doubt my own observation. I am given a cold, stone room with two beds. I have no idea where I am and I do not feel very happy. After an hour I am awoken by a laughing man, who introduces himself as a German reporter, and who takes the other bed. He was on the same plane as I, but his car crashed halfway to Jerusalem. Drearily I continue my sleep.

Friday, April 7. I open my eyes to a hilly landscape, replete with rocks and bushes, on which the rain is pouring down. Feeling miserable, without even a coat, I walk out into the street under my umbrella. It seems to be some kind of Sunday—there is not even bus service. Thank God, ten minutes later some ungodly, clandestine taxi catches up with me, a rattling Dodge with eight people on board already, driven by a one-legged chauffeur. The chatter in Hebrew soothes me like a massage, and in the King David Hotel, where I am dropped off, I finally relax a bit.

The hotel is located next to Herod's tomb, on the edge of a vast valley: that is Jordan. The opulent lounge is filled with Americans, probably Jewish pilgrims; extravagantly formal waiters are striding over the carpets. It is the kind of hotel every city in the world has. Inventor: Cesare Ritz. In different weather the back of the hotel probably provides a splendid view of the Arab city, now practically invisible in the pouring rain. In the past, this hotel was on the west side of Jerusalem; after the division of 1948 it became the most eastern part of the new Jerusalem built by the Israelis.

After an hour I suddenly know innumerable Israeli officials, and reporters, people from radio and TV, from all over the world.

People only speak about Eichmann while shrugging their shoulders. Nobody talks about him as a person or about his crimes; only Israel's authority to try him is considered. Most doubt this to be right in a legal sense, but naturally, they think the Jews are absolutely right. Almost all oppose the death penalty for Eichmann—that would not be wise. Eichmann himself does not matter to anybody. The ambiance is matter-of-fact and businesslike. I ask an American reporter, who has been here for a couple of days already, whether the atmosphere among the Israelis is tense or even dangerous. He has to laugh, takes another bite of his matzo, and says that he was a censor during the Korean War, and that he has a keen eye for letters that have been opened: some of the letters he has received here in Israel had been opened. I then also order matzo with chicken, and coffee. The waiter refuses, politely but firmly, to give me the milk I request: if a soul drinks milk in his coffee while eating meat, be it poultry or beef, then that soul will be eradicated from its peoples. That is what he said, in so many words. I will buy a Bible. The Scripture is indispensable in this country, both as a cookbook and as a travel guide.

In the afternoon it stops raining. The city remains deserted. Even the cafés are closed because, I have been told, today is the last day of Passover, meaning that it is actually Saturday, here meaning that it is Sunday today. In the embassy Jaguar we go with a group of people to a high point outside the city—and there the panorama of the supernatural unfolds. Bordered by hills, dotted with churches, cloisters, towers, and minarets, lies the old Jerusalem between its walls, in the valley. Underneath the cedars on the slope on the opposite side: the garden of Gethsemane; a little farther lies Golgotha. The Mount of Olives. In this valley Abraham laid his son on the altar; over there, on Mount Zion, David founded his kingdom. From there Mary ascended to heaven. But also in the middle of the city, the gold dome of the Mosque of Omar shines, built on top of the stables of Solomon. It is there that Muhammad ascended to heaven. In the same valley the Messiah of the orthodox Jews will appear.

Why all this, precisely here? Speechless, I look around. What makes this place so special? Sacred land of three religions—a fertile land indeed. On the Ebstorf world map of the thirteenth century, Jerusalem is put exactly in the middle. Since on the surface of a sphere any point may be called the center, on the Earth's surface Jerusalem is the prime candidate: it is the religious pole to which most compasses point. Dante even discovered the religious "antipole": after the ninth circle of Hell, he and Virgil left the inside of the Earth diametrically opposite Jerusalem; one glance at the globe shows that that is in the Pacific Ocean. I think I am going to buy a globe and fix it along this axis.

Diametrically opposite the nuclear mushrooms of the South Seas, I am looking at Golgotha. If I wanted to go there, a thirty-minute walk, I would have to maneuver for about a week to obtain a second passport, one without Israeli stamps in it, to allow me through the Mandelbaum Gate into the Arab city; I would also have to get shots against smallpox and be baptized. In order to return (but it is not certain that one returns from Golgotha at age thirty-three), I would have to take the train to Amman, the plane to Cyprus, from Cyprus another plane to Tel Aviv, and from Tel Aviv the train to Jerusalem.

Turning around, I see a white Arab village in the valley in the distance. That is Bethlehem, says the ambassador. Behind me I hear a man say that Eichmann was brought, in secrecy and anaesthetized, to his cell in Jerusalem two nights ago.

Saturday, April 8. The border between Israel and Jordan is formed by the fossilized frontline of 1948. Jerusalem lies at the top of a jagged bulge, surrounded on three sides by Arab territory, twenty-five kilometers from the northern-most point of the Dead Sea. But if one wants to see the Dead Sea, one has to make a half-day detour by car to reach the southern-most point.

Two hours southwest of Jerusalem, in a vast, slightly hilly landscape, lies Kiryat Gat, named after the Philistine Gath, the birthplace of Goliath. In a circle spread over a vast area, one finds settlements everywhere in the hills; rows of small white houses, which are irresistibly reminiscent of the concentration camps. But for the inhabitants they mean freedom at last! What kind of freedom? A cheerless freedom in an unknown country? In each of these villages immigrants from yet another country live their own lives and speak their own languages: there are Moroccans over there, Russians over there, Yemenites over there, Poles over there, Persians over there. But in the center of the circle there is a square nucleus with shops, schools, and recreation centers. Only that nucleus is Israel, the mortar, the melting pot, where people meet, where children play, where they are taught in the common language, Hebrew. That is the way Israel's dramatic experiment, thought to be impossible, works, and it seems to be successful. Here one can learn the meaning of "courage from desperation." It is Sabbath: not a soul outside. Seeing the motionless white villages in the endless landscape, where Joshua once made the sun stop, I am filled with awe, while at the same time desperate desertedness is creeping up on me, which is hiding behind this pioneer spirit: the double face of the persecutor.

We eat in Beersheba; then we travel again, an hour southward, and we are in the desert. Beersheba, the capital of the Negev, was founded long ago by Abraham, king of the nomads, who dug springs for his people. Now tractors rattle to the left and right of the asphalt roads, but biblical times still exist, in the shape of the Bedouin. Like the black cocoons of giant insects, their tents are up on the slopes of the desert, which we are entering now, eastward. Their faces barely perceptible in their garments, they herd their flocks of sheep and black goats, which can be seen even miles away, as if drawn in India ink against the yellow stone. A small Bedouin boy passes along the road on a camel, playing his flute. The women hide their faces when we pass. Still deeper into the desert, where nothing has grown in a long time and where everything has turned into a shriveled-up, hilly landscape, I suddenly see a Bedouin, a small dot in the distance, walking from nowhere to nowhere. While the guide is talking scornfully about their laziness, about their filthiness, and their polygamy, I can hardly hold back my tears, overcome by emotion. Maybe people can be divided into those who mount tractors and try to make the best of the situation and those who give up immediately and just continue their lonely walk through the desert.

Here and there the desert is in bloom: yellow flowers sprouting from yellow stone. We pass kibbutz Dimona: rows of small white houses, inhabited by the strongest. Now, in April, we have already taken off our jackets and we are puffing in the heat; in the summer the climate must resemble that of Venus! Somewhat later a conglomerate of somber buildings dawns on the southern horizon. The guide is silently humming and looking through the windshield; but even without the heavily armed soldiers, who suddenly appear here and there, the more intelligent ones among us have recognized the nuclear power plant. A Dane in our group asks what kind of buildings those are, on the horizon. The guide smiles. "A textile factory," he says. The Scandinavian stares at the horizon, in amazement. Crazy Jews, he is thinking.

The guide prefers to talk about the road: more than sixty miles from Beersheba to the Dead Sea, built by five thousand laborers, under the merciless conditions of burning sun and shooting Arabs. Toward the end of the journey we are starting to descend, and an inspiring view opens up. We get out of the car and find ourselves in an extraterrestrial silence. Some twenty miles away are the red-copper mountains of Jordan; between us and those mountains, surrounded by an inhuman white landscape of salt rocks, thousands of feet deep, lies a breathless aquamarine: the Dead Sea. If there is any name that was fittingly given, it is this one. Here, at the lowest point on Earth, twelve hundred feet below sea level, something terrible happened. Death has taken shape. Here the fist came down: the place where we are is called Sodom. Under a damp fog the sea lies dying in the deep, and being turned into salt, also when no one is looking. We are silent and stare in the dead, silent, sweating agony. Is this what he had wanted to be, Eichmann?

Sunday, April 9. On this first day of work, the engine is getting into gear. There is pushing and shouting in the pressroom, where we are given our passes to the courthouse, cards for telex, telephone, and telegrams. We also receive a couple of pounds of documents, from the indictment to a list of SS rankings, and a set of elegant plastic headphones, for the translations—manufactured by Philips, but the brand name has been removed since the company no longer works for Israel. The Arab nations forced them to choose. We sign a declaration, in which we commit ourselves to submitting our texts other than about Eichmann to a military censor. I feel that I will forget about that.

The building in which the trial will take place lies in the center of modern Jerusalem. It had been under construction as a House of the People, Beit Ha'am, for years, but was finished with the trial in mind, which will take place in the auditorium of the recreation center. There is an active army of at least one hundred military men and police. They are everywhere, with their automatic guns ready (these are so excellent that the German army is buying them by the thousands). With their fingers on the trigger, they are on duty on the flat roof of the brand-new building, and also on the roofs of the surrounding houses. Near all the entrances in the roadblock there are groups of Jews talking: workers from Jerusalem, black women from North Africa, biblical figures from Yemen, European immigrants, and unkempt Orthodox Jews with black hats, caftans (a sort of tailor-made jacket reaching over the knees, made from the same material as the pants), unruly beards, and corkscrew curls over their cheeks.

Upon presentation of my pass I am allowed past the first roadblock, and I arrive at a row of bathing cubicles. I open one of the doors and am greeted by a policeman. He frisks me from head to toe, with a preference for my armpits. After distrustfully having examined my lighter, he lets me out through the backdoor. Then I can see the madhouse in full operation. Reporters and military personnel are running in and out of the building, girls are carrying cases with orange juice, workers are hoisting incomprehensible machines up into the windows. Inside, too, they are still putting in the finishing touches. A post office has already been furnished. In the pressroom, which looks like a classroom for four hundred students, TV sets are being installed, on which the trial will be shown uninterruptedly. I am walking around like a stranger in Babylon.

When I leave in the evening, the building is bathed in spotlights. It is apparently a hotspot in the city: in front of the gate there are large groups of boys with radios under their shirts. From their bodies dance music is jangling while they are trying to reach for their girlfriends. When they see me leaving the building, they shout: "Shalom, Doctor Servatius!" It could become the title of a top hit. On the roof, the guard is standing among the stars.

Monday, April 10. During the coming eight months the sun will be shining. I have spent the entire day in the yard underneath the palm trees, reading and working. My hostel is quite to my liking now. The grumpy old man from the first day has developed into a friendly Romanian, with whom I talk about Bucharest and about the curious habit of the women there to go braless.

Tuesday, April 11. The courtroom does not get any quieter. Almost no one saw how he appeared from out of the wall into his glass cage. His gestures, both stiff and supple at the same time, give away the fact that he wore an officer's uniform half of his life. Compared to last year's last picture he has aged. He is wearing a dark suit and glasses. Two or three times he glances into the courtroom, with an emotionless face, and then does not do it again during the entire session. He is seated left, on the podium in the modern auditorium, lit by soft neon lights. The wall paneling has holes for invisible TV cameras. Behind a long table, with their backs to the room, Servatius and his assistant are seated, next to the public prosecutor and four assistants. The chairs of the three judges are on a platform opposite them. When the judges enter, Eichmann quickly and obediently stands at attention. The president asks him whether he is Adolf Eichmann, and he answers curtly "Jawohl." He offers the same answer when asked if he accepts Servatius as his counsel for the defense.

In plaintive Hebrew the president begins to read the accusation aloud, point by point, waiting for the translation into German every time. Eichmann listens, standing at attention, his head somewhat to the right, pulling with his mouth from time to time, but moving less than his guard. One of the guards cannot keep his eyes off the back of Eichmann's head. I know what he is looking for. I cannot find it either. In fifteen points the terrible indictment is pounding down on him. Twelve of them carry the death penalty. Millions of Jews gassed in Auschwitz; hundreds of thousands of dead in the work camps; forced abortions on Jewish women during all stages of pregnancy; deportation of half a million Poles and fourteen thousand Slovenes; the killing of one hundred children from Lidice. There is no end. At the fourth point he assumes an easier position. When the president speaks, he looks at the president; when the interpreter speaks, he looks at the interpreter. He does not show any sign of changes in his state of mind. It is as though he does not understand German either. But when the president finally asks him whether he has understood the indictment, he again answers curtly "Jawohl." He is probably the only person in the world who can say this.

While the first reporters are running to the phones, the greatest public lesson in world history begins. Servatius, who looks like a reliable doctor from the countryside, raises an objection. Polite and articulate, holding back for the translation every time, he calls the court incompetent and prejudiced. All the judges were born in Germany, and all fled from Hitler to Israel in 1933. Eichmann blows his nose, and now I can see that his bulky, stiff hands are trembling. Bending politely, quoting Heine, Servatius talks about the desirability of an international court of justice, and about the impossibility for him to call witnesses. They would automatically be arrested in Israel for their own crimes. When he starts talking about responsibility without guilt, he is entering dangerous territory. He asks how one man can pay for the death of almost an entire people, and for the crimes of an entire country.

While the trial proceeds like an endless train, I leave the room. With the transistor in my ears, which allows me to follow everything, I look outside. Cameramen are filming the motley Jewish crowd behind the fences. Mounted police are dispersing groups of shouting youngsters. My thought is that the worst punishment for Eichmann would be immediate discharge.

Going down the steps, I now hear the translation of the public prosecutor's words. He says that Israel is the only country in the world that wants to try Eichmann, and that here no judge can be impartial. The judge that would be impartial here would be incompetent. The point is not impartiality, but justice. With every corner I turn I lose the radio connection for a moment.

In the insane excitement of the pressroom, I see Eichmann sneeze on the TV screen. I think: he is sneezing.

Wednesday, April 12. With horror I think back to last night, when five hundred reporters dashed to the booths to telegraph, to phone, to telex their messages across the globe. In the immediately ensuing bedlam, and to everyone's dismay, the maximum for telegrams was set at two hundred words, and six minutes for phone calls. At home at summits and in revolutions, most appeared to be at ease in the shouting and pushing, but for a simple writer this was awful. Used to taking his manuscripts comfortably through the sun to his publisher, who welcomes him with a glass of sherry, he now had to push Poles and Brazilians aside and hit his fist on the table to get Israeli operators to work. Six o'clock was the time for my phone call: at eight I was at my wits' end. Furious, chain-smoking, I looked at the reporters who had already sent their articles: you could pick them out by their unworldly calm, which radiated from their faces in a disgusting way. I was told that for a reporter the quality of his article is less important than that it appears in the newspaper on time. In that sense I showed myself to be a good reporter—at ten o'clock, I could finally, in jubilation, run to a phone booth, throwing some South Americans to the ground, and shout my text piecemeal to Amsterdam, with an Italian in the cabin next to mine bellowing "Pronto! Pronto!," and on the other side a chirping Japanese lady of the *Asahi Shimboen*, circulation ten million. And then I too walked on winged feet through the Beit Ha'am. Not until a couple of hours later, drinking Israeli cognac in a basement bar filled with impressive Israeli paratroopers, did I realize how much I had failed. It would take me until today to understand why.

The effect that Eichmann has had on the world cannot be reduced to his actions alone. It can also be explained by his invisibility. Before the war he was an invisible SD clerk. During the war he was an invisibly operating SS officer. After the war he was an invisible, hiding Nazi. During the past year he was an invisible prisoner in Israel. Theology has described the effect of invisibility on people. The image of Satan that the press has created out of Eichmann in the last few months can be more easily approached theologically than psychologically. Servatius had every reason to note that the press is not the court. And now Eichmann has suddenly become visible—in excess of theology in Jerusalem: Bethlehem and Golgotha, visible from the roofs. Everybody is preoccupied with this fact, but hardly anyone dares write about it.

But with Eichmann the theological effect has disappeared with his apparition. He turns out to be human: a somewhat grubby man with a cold, wearing glasses. In order to reestablish some of the past effect, a new invisibility must be designed: for example, that he was a member of Himmler's inner circle. I have not met anyone here yet who is not preoccupied with this kind of mental exercise, intended to keep the image of Eichmann as Satan alive for the world. It is in vain, and it will seem more and more so. Similarly, Eichmann will not be able to satisfy the world's desire. He will become smaller and smaller. The day will come that he has disappeared, and then he will be what he has always been: an errant spot on our retinas.

Today the courtroom is half empty, and to observe him well, I go sit in the front row, ten feet away from him. He is more relaxed than yesterday. When he enters, he gives me a brief smile. It gave me the fright of my life—but his smile was not for me, but for Servatius, seated exactly between us. Some time later, while awaiting the arrival of the court, he talks with Servatius via a microphone. Then I have a good view of his eyes. People here wrote that he has snake eyes (*France Soir*), and also that each of his eyes is a gas chamber (*Libération*). But in truth they are soft and somewhat velvety, which is only more horrifying. Their expression freezes when he listens to the public prosecutor, who is continuing his legal plea on the competence of the court for the whole day today. Contrary to those of his three judges, Eichmann's eyes do not leave the prosecutor for a second, hour after hour. Sometimes they suddenly shoot sideways, in some sort of a tic. Then his head shudders for a moment, and he sucks his cheeks in, which makes him pull his mouth to the left. In moments like these, he is somewhat like the Eichmann we would like to see: an inexplicably merciless face, sending shivers up my spine—a shattered face, simultaneously evoking strong pity. Yesterday I was seated too far away to notice this.

When the session is adjourned, I find myself in a conversation with a Jewish journalist of Dutch origin in the cafeteria. He tells me that he was comparing Eichmann's face to those of the people in the courtroom, and that an important difference struck him.

What was missing in Eichmann's face was the "Jewish soul." But then he realized there were also many non-Jews in the room. That had amazed him. "I am not afraid to say this to you, even though you are only half Jewish. I am prepared to repeat it for your colleague, who is not Jewish at all." And so he does, which prompts my colleague to say that he met Jewish officers during the Suez Crisis who had faces similar to Eichmann's. The response: "They must have originated from the Orient."

Sometimes I get the impression that everyone here is anti-Semitic, Jews and non-Jews alike. Another Dutch journalist, very Aryan, approaches me to ask whether I, as a half Jew, *recognize* much here in Israel. Everyone seems to have made a mental note of the fact that I am half Jewish. When I say that I was raised by my Aryan father, he starts in on blood and heredity, saying that according to the Talmud I am a Jew. I say that he himself would have had corkscrew curls over his ears had he been raised in the ultra-Orthodox area of Me'ah Shearim, but he, distressed, doubts that. Finally he tries to get out of it by saying that he is just a simple Dutch country boy and probably too dumb to understand certain things, which I confirm.

In the afternoon we learn that on the front page of the newspapers Eichmann's name has been replaced by Yuri Gagarin, who was also over Jerusalem during the opening of the trial, in space. But he will not be able to satisfy the world's desire either.

Thursday, April 13. Today no trial: a commemorative day for heroes and martyrs. To attend a celebration we drive to Yad Mordechai, on the Egyptian border near Gaza. This kibbutz is known for its inhabitants, survivors of the Polish and Russian ghettos, and for its battle during the War of Independence in 1948. Twice bombed and finally razed by tanks, it became the grave of dozens of Jews, who had recently escaped the massacres of Warsaw and Vilna. We are introduced to the man who was commander-in-chief at that time, Shimon Avidan: an old peasant with a curiously crooked face. The Egyptian commander-in-chief in this part of the front in those days was Colonel Gamal Abdel Nasser, who mentions Avidan in one of his writings. While Avidan is talking with us, his eyes constantly wander to the modern prism binoculars hanging on my belly.

Yad Mordechai is a true border kibbutz: half farm, half fortress. Everyone can fight if necessary, the women too; there is an abundance of weapons now, and around the central buildings (the conference room, the automated soup kitchen, the daycare centers, where the children are collectively raised), bunkers have been built everywhere in the slopes. The border is five hundred yards away. There the fertile land instantly changes into white sand. Deep into the dried up Gaza Strip I see, through my enviable binoculars, a light-green wadi with palm trees. I am trying to find my Bedouin, to no avail.

Over the roads adorned with red flags, the comrades of the national Communist Mapan party walk to their meeting point. On top of a steep hill, in front of a water tank that has fallen to the side and has been shot to pieces, there is a gigantic worker in bronze with a hand grenade in his fist, in socialist-realist style. Taken there by buses, people from neighboring kibbutzim are also coming together, and on long benches they are awaiting the sunset. Just like every other day, this commemorative day starts with the appearance of the first stars. To the side, underneath the trees, groups of soldiers are lazily stretched out, their automatic guns ready to fire on the ground next to them. Everywhere boys and girls of the Mapan youth are gathering, in their blue overalls and red scarves.

While dusk is settling in, I get involved in a conversation with one of them. When I start in on Eichmann, he shrugs his shoulders. From his broken English I understand that he views the trial as the nagging of the old folks. Having grown up in a moneyless, semi-military society with red flags, raised in a collective daycare center, without cigarettes or cinemas, and with the enemy at the end of the field, he cannot get excited about the official misery of his parents. He thinks that it is about time for them to shut up about it.

My next conversation partner clarifies what the Mapan boy means. "We want our children not to forget and not to forgive either," he says, "we want them to hate Germany until they die."

He himself was the only one of his family to escape from the ghetto of Warsaw. He fought for a while with the partisans and then in the Red Army. I remind him that many Jews are opposed to the Eichmann trial because they fear anti-Semitism will be fed by it. They believe the word "Jew" should be used as little as possible. He is furious, saying that that is the old ghetto mentality again, which the Jews should shed once and for all. He mentions the Dutch Jews, who allowed themselves to be slaughtered like sheep. I ask him what they should have done, rounded up in Amsterdam, a city surrounded by fields. He does not want to hear about it. "What did we do in Warsaw? Could the Dutch Jews not have broken through to the sea, to a seaport? Could they not have tried to reach England?" Hearing this makes me suddenly understand the ubiquitous indifference toward *The Diary of Anne Frank* in Israel. That too represents the ghetto mentality.

With a burst of applause the heroes of Warsaw are greeted on the podium. Ten aging men in civilian suits, looking somewhat bewilderedly into the cheering crowd. Among them is a forty-five-year-old balding man with a black patch over his left eye; his right, amazingly blue and clear, takes in the world. That is the legendary General Moshe Dayan, commander-in-chief of the Israeli armed forces during the Suez Crisis, and the idol of his soldiers. A little later, with a roll of drums and the blowing of trumpets, the Mapan youth come down the hill, and while the night is coming quickly now, and on the slopes around us the crickets are chirping, an old man with a white beard gives a speech. He was once the leader of the Polish Jews. All I can understand is the word "Eichmann." Meanwhile I see that couples are breaking away from the rows in the back and disappearing into the darkness of the kibbutz.

After an allegorical ballet performance, we talk with Ruzka Korchak, the leader of the revolt in the ghetto of Vilna. She does not even come up to my shoulders, and in 1942 she must have been twenty at most. I will never forget her face. While she is telling us that they did not fight for their lives, but to determine their own way of dying, a pain appears in her face that I would not have thought possible in a human being, miles away from crying, a memory of despair and death, and she is still alive; a pain that is indescribable, at least with my pen. I turn away and think about Eichmann. I am thinking: "Give him to me here and now, and I will destroy him with my own hands."

Friday, April 14. Slowly everybody here is becoming schizophrenic about Eichmann. We know what he did, although it still has to be proven, but in the cage we see a lonely, dying man. Do we hate him? Do we love him? During the day everyone is changing into him; at night groups of reporters, in all the bars and cafés, are attempting to come to terms with it. Eichmann has become a disease. Like a helpless swastika-cross spider taken from its web, he listens to the public prosecutor. He only lowers his eyes to blow his nose, and it is clear that he can hardly understand what is going on. If they had put an empty SS uniform in the cage, with an SS hat hovering above it, they would have had a defendant of greater reality. When they arrested him in Argentina and put an SS hat on to identify him, the moment of truth was nearer than now, when the breathing, digesting, sneezing man appears in the courtroom. I have asked people who saw him in the concentration camps how much he has changed. All they could remember was a hat, shiny boots, and a pair of square riding pants.

During the session he has already almost been forgotten. The fat court officer, who announces the arrival of the court with an unintelligible shout, is more important than he is. From behind a table covered with books, Gideon Hausner continues his technical plea about the competence of the court. With innumerable precedents of details he is trying to create a super precedent, which would allow for a defendant to be convicted for acts that were not punishable at the time they were committed. It is still about defendant X; the Eichmann trial has yet to begin. This is a feast for the lawyers.

Although Hausner takes on the poses of a brilliant speaker, he is not. He is also hindered by the obligatory pauses for the translation. He is of Polish origin, forty-six years old, and already balding. His mouth is grim, his blue eyes closed under heavy, raised eyebrows: the face of a man who has made up his mind. He seldom looks at Eichmann. When their eyes do meet, he immediately turns his eyes away. Four of his fingertips have small band-aids.

Judge Moshe Landau looks at Eichmann just as he looks at anybody else in the courtroom. It seldom happens. He is forty-nine years old, but looks sixty. Everyone, including the defense, admires him without reservation. If there is anything beyond all doubt, it is that he will lead this trial fairly. His silence, his listening to Hausner and Servatius, his hand brushing over his chin, his friendly interruptions, and his explanations will hit Eichmann harder than Hausner's outstretched index finger—if there is anything that could hit him, which is not the case.

Judge Benjamin Halevi, also born in Germany, looks younger than his fifty-one years. He has thick gray hair, cold eyes, and a cold mouth. He regularly introduces something, as opposed to Judge Yitzhak Raveh, who from time to time gives the impression of being on the verge of falling asleep. Even a foreigner can hear the German accent in the Hebrew of them all.

When Hausner is finally done, by the end of the morning, Servatius still has the right of reply. He says that Eichmann, freed from his Nazi oath, has become a peace-loving citizen—and a baffled buzzing fills the courtroom. Even some tentative whistling can be heard. Landau lifts his head for a moment, and it is immediately quiet. Ten reporters leave the room to send this remark out into the world. The two inspectors sitting in their light blue suits on the podium, writing down everything that is happening in the room, are becoming increasingly observant. Eichmann does not show any sign of emotion.

Saturday, April 15. When I come home in the evening, there is a man on the lawn in the dark, following me with his eyes until I am inside. In the entrance hall of the bunker-like annex under the palm trees, there is again a man in the dark: his right hand is in the pocket of his overcoat. He recognizes me and says goodnight. They are the bodyguards of Servatius, who sleeps in the room next to mine.

As I am writing this, in the small lounge, Servatius is eating behind me, being interviewed by an American journalist. His assis-

tant, at my table, is in discussion with a Dutch journalist, an Israeli, and the landlord. He is twenty-nine. His name is
Wechtenbruch. His hair is short, and he is more intelligent than
friendly. He has spoken with Eichmann for months, every day for
at least three hours, and he says Eichmann is the most ordinary
man one can imagine: "improperly normal." A million others
would have done the same in his position. A British TV camera-
man feels the need to take the German people under his protection, but Wechtenbruch says that it is "unfortunately true."

At the bar, Servatius's female assistant is telling Eichmann
stories to a judge from Milwaukee and to an Italian reporter. I
overhear her say that he has requested permission to hang himself, that he once fainted at a bullfight, and that he asked her for
a mirror during his transfer to Jerusalem: he had not seen himself
for a year.

Sunday, April 16. The entire day the talks about the competence of
the court continue, in the lounge, on the lawn in the sun, and
underneath the palm trees. Most are hoping for a negative decision, which would be best for everyone, especially Israel. Then
extradition to Poland could be the next step, a trial of ten days,
followed by the gallows within twenty-four hours, facing Auschwitz.

But in a Dutch newspaper I read that a famous minister said
during a meeting in Amsterdam: "Eichmann is the man who has
become a non-man, a phenomenon of absolute godlessness and
non-humanness." If it could only be that simple! The remark is as
religious as it is fatal. If there is *anything* we can hold against
Eichmann, it is not his belief (he believed: in the führer, in the
Final Solution, in the Jews, and in what not), but his doubt. Exactly the doubt of any "absoluteness," also the absolute godlessness. Eichmann himself would be much uplifted by the minister's
words.

In the afternoon by Jaguar off to the lush valley of Elah, where
David slew Goliath. After eight days of sunshine all the flowers
have practically withered already. Then Jerusalem's nightlife. Although the four-thousand-year-old city is one of the oldest in the

world, mentioned in hieroglyphs and cuneiform, it is still as provincial as Haarlem:* just slightly bigger than absolute boredom. The ideal city to work in. It is the boredom of any seat of government, here amplified by the murderous influence of the religious part of the population. The absence of outdoor cafés is terrible. They say Tel Aviv is different. It is whispered that there the buses run on Sabbath, with Baal's servants behind the wheels. Jerusalem does offer unprecedented opportunities for avowed Sunday haters. The day before yesterday I met a Dutch major of the UN contingent: on Fridays, the Muhammadan day of rest, this enviable man comes in his white Jeep to the Jewish city. On Saturdays he goes to the Arab city, thus avoiding Sundays altogether—of course, nobody has ever heard of such novelties as *Sunday*.

Three main streets in the center form an equilateral triangle, within which city life takes place. Here one can find the excellent bar where the Dutch guest is greeted with a "Good evening, sir" in badly pronounced Dutch, just as the Russian guest will hear this in Russian, and where one can learn the most priceless dirty words from drunken English journalists. Here there are taxi stands and the Arab restaurants, the stores, the promenade, the dark jazz cellar filled with entertainers, the espresso bar, and the Italian restaurant, even more expensive than the other restaurants in this most expensive country in the world. This expensiveness is mirrored in an agreeable and total lack of luxury, but not in poverty. It is the atmosphere of a Communist country, but without the pressure that poisons life in East Germany, Czechoslovakia, or Romania. In short, this is the most agreeable atmosphere imaginable, currently probably to be found elsewhere only in Cuba. But one day all-destroying prosperity will likely make its appearance here. When will a politician dare speak out *against* prosperity? And then not as a temporary measure, in order to promise a greater prosperity, but once and for all, because it is a disgrace—as is poverty.

*Haarlem is the capital of the province of North Holland, and the birthplace of the author.

Monday, April 17. In a short declaration at the opening of the session, Landau decides that the court is competent. Thus ends trial X and begins the Eichmann trial. Concerning the prejudice of the judges, he says that when in the judge's seat they do not cease to be people of flesh and blood, with human feelings, but that it is *always* their job to fight their feelings—if not, a judge would never be able to preside over a murder case or any other serious crime. Immediately he asks Eichmann to stand up—and then the following dialogue develops:

"Did you hear the indictment on the first day of this case?"
"Jawohl."
"Are you guilty or not guilty on the first count?"
"Not guilty in the sense of the indictment."
"Are you guilty or not guilty on the second count?"
"Not guilty in the sense of the indictment."
"Are you guilty or not guilty on the third count?"
"Not guilty in the sense of the indictment."
"Are you guilty or not guilty on the fourth count?"
"Not guilty in the sense of the indictment."
"Are you guilty or not guilty on the fifth count?"
"Not guilty in the sense of the indictment."
"Are you guilty or not guilty on the sixth count?"
"Not guilty in the sense of the indictment."
"Are you guilty or not guilty on the seventh count?"
"Not guilty in the sense of the indictment."
"Are you guilty or not guilty on the eighth count?"
"Not guilty in the sense of the indictment."
"Are you guilty or not guilty on the ninth count?"
"Not guilty in the sense of the indictment."
"Are you guilty or not guilty on the tenth count?"
"Not guilty in the sense of the indictment."
"Are you guilty or not guilty on the eleventh count?"
"Not guilty in the sense of the indictment."
"Are you guilty or not guilty on the twelfth count?"
"Not guilty in the sense of the indictment."
"Are you guilty or not guilty on the thirteenth count?"

"Not guilty in the sense of the indictment."
"Are you guilty or not guilty on the fourteenth count?"
"Not guilty in the sense of the indictment."
"Are you guilty or not guilty on the fifteenth count?"
"Not guilty in the sense of the indictment."

The courtroom listens on the edge of their seats. Neither Eich-mann's nor Landau's face shows any trace of emotion. Eichmann speaks softly, rather quickly, his tone increasingly routine-like. Everybody is hoping for at least one "guilty." (When I commented to a female reporter what a relief that would have been for us and the world, she said: "Don't forget he has children.")

Then Gideon Hausner stands up, never to sit down again the entire day. He addresses the court with "Judges in Israel," and he calls on the six million dead to speak through him. He speaks of Pharaoh and Haman, and says that the most horrific acts of Nero, Attila, and Genghis Khan pale in comparison with the horror of the extermination that will be shown during this trial. I do not think he should speak in Eichmann's vein, and I quickly look at the man in the terrarium. No emotions on his face—but with all that I am I know that he feels flattered: he would prefer to be more terrible than Genghis Khan than to be public prosecutor in criminal case # 40/61, which is the official designation. Hausner is more effective when he talks about the modern killers, who do not leave their desks, and that he only knows with certainty of one case in which Eichmann killed someone with his own hands: when he beat a Jewish boy to death for stealing a couple of peaches from his garden in Budapest.

The room is shivering more now than when the abstract, by now half-mystical number of six million was mentioned. Hausner is not proving anything yet—he is only filling in the background. Exactly as this did not happen in Nuremberg, he doubts whether this trial will lay bare fully the roots of evil; it will remain the domain of historians, sociologists, writers, and psychologists to explain to the world what has been done to it, he says. He appar-ently still believes in an "explanation," while in the same breath speaks of "breaking through the window of human logic." Behind this reality there is no more explanation. It is in itself an explanation of what man is. It is the final word thus far.

He then talks about the effect Hitler had on his surroundings; he cites Goethe on the "demon personality," and deals with the sources of anti-Semitism. He hardly adds anything new to what has been said about these things. But maybe that is not his intention; it is his intention to disclose, to give the world a memory. At the end of his introduction he quotes from Hitler's testament. A few days before his death, when the Russian cannons could be heard in his Berlin bunker, Hitler obliged the German people to maintain painfully the racial laws and to resist mercilessly the "world poisoner" of all peoples: international Jewry.

Hausner then deals with the setup of the terror system, about which I have already written. I stopped in the year 1938. At the start of the war, in 1939, Himmler divided his SS into twelve *Hauptämter* [main departments]. One of these was the Reichssicherheitshauptamt (RSHA) under Heydrich. In this center, which would soon manage all of Europe and have agents all over the world, all the police and intelligence services were organized. Since Hitler would concentrate on warfare from then on, Himmler's and Heydrich's power grew immensely. The RSHA had seven offices; one of these was the SD, which during the war alone already had about two hundred thousand employees. A special section of the SD spied on the spy service of the army, the Abwehr under Canaris. Office IV was the Geheime Staatspolizei-Amt [Secret State Police Department], Gestapa, managed by SS-Gruppenführer Heinrich Müller, Eichmann's direct boss. Division IV B was the Gestapo; subdivision IV B1 was the section for Catholic affairs, IV B2 for Protestant affairs, IV B3 for all sorts of religious sects, and IV B4 for Jewish affairs. This stood under the command of Eichmann. It was a sly move by Heydrich to define administratively this gigantic office, which soon needed its own building, as an insignificant part of the whole. Who would assume that such a sub division, IV B4, administered the extermination of millions? This secrecy also allowed Eichmann to work in almost perfect anonymity. For example, it is possible that even someone like Göbbels did not know his name. For the same reasons, his rank was never higher than *Obersturmbannführer* (lieutenant colonel), but his power was greater than that of cabinet members, the Reich's commissioners and army generals.

To finish this paragraph, Hausner extensively deals with the most important weapon of the SS: the concentration camps, and how these were purposely geared toward the total numbing of man, through hunger, torture, or continuous execution scenes. In the sewing room it happened that someone would, by coincidence, be given the clothes of his murdered wife or children, to remove the star and to fill the bullet holes. For a moment his eyes would glisten, but it would go away immediately; he would not scream, he would not go crazy. Numbed, he would continue fixing the clothes for a German woman or for German children.

Hausner's description of Eichmann's life is the same as what I wrote earlier. He speaks of his intermittently violent and soothing methods toward the Austrian and Czech Jews. When he says that Eichmann hit the leader of the Jews in Vienna in the face, the motionless man in his cage takes a piece of paper to scribble something down.

Hour after hour, Hausner continues his first survey of the terrain, the exploration of which will probably take months: the actions of Eichmann's representatives, whom he sent to Croatia, Greece, Denmark, Russia, the Netherlands, Bulgaria, Luxembourg, and many other countries; the way he personally, as *Großmeister der Vernichtung* [grandmaster of the extermination], headed a select group of bandits in Hungary, in 1944, and within nine months transported nearly half a million Jews to the gas chambers. It was to be expected that Hausner would emphasize this especially, since here Eichmann could not use the traditional excuse of "an order is an order." On the contrary: in October Himmler ordered him to stop the deportations. Even the *Reichsführer SS* understood then that the war was going to end badly. Because he got the idea that the allies would be willing to negotiate with him, but not with Hitler, and that he therefore had to succeed Hitler, he tried to erase traces wherever he could. Eichmann proceeded to deport the Jews against Himmler's orders. First in stuffed freight trains, ninety Jews per car. At every crossing, the dead were discharged, and those who had gone crazy were shot dead. And finally on foot: death marches unlike any the world had ever seen before. Auschwitz commandant Höss called them inhumane.

By the time Hausner announces to the court many examples of how Eichmann, despite these mass actions, still found time to make the emigration of this or that Jew impossible, everyone can only stare in disbelief at the man in his dark suit. Is it the same man? Nobody can get it into their heads. He listens motionlessly, every once in a while moving a finger of his folded hand.

Hausner is now talking about the "The Final Solution to the Jewish Question," that is the killing of all the Jews, decided on January 20, 1942, and of which Eichmann was put in charge, with only Heydrich and Himmler between him and Hitler. He organized the deportation of the ghettos. He determined a suitable spot for a concentration camp near the Polish village of Auschwitz. He decided which gas to use (Zyklon B, an insecticide). He observed mass executions of women and children in Russia. He watched as hundreds of naked Jews were led into the gas chambers. He was there when, after their death, their gold teeth were hacked out of their jaws. He had them write postcards beforehand, and he had them sent months later, in order to squash the rumors about the extermination of people.

Yet, next to me a journalist has fallen asleep. I leave the courtroom and go watch TV between the rattling typewriters, while Hausner is giving a survey of the extermination of Jews in Poland and Russia. Close-ups of Eichmann are interspersed with those of Hausner and also with faces from the room. Suddenly I notice some people are crying. I can even see who they are, but we are the only ones to see it: it is a closed circuit, and there is no TV in Israel. Then the camera unexpectedly focuses on the sleeping man I was sitting next to. It sticks to the image as though it cannot believe it. Then the picture abruptly switches to Judge Moshe Landau's face. His face does not give anything away.

Tuesday, April 18. Today, for the first time, the soldiers functioning as porters and ushers are dressed in their khaki summer uniforms.

It is warm, and Eichmann's cold is finally over. His white handkerchief stays in his left inside pocket today. "He is well again," we say to each other.

With one more exposé on the concentration camps and a sketch of the cultural wounds inflicted upon the Jewish people, Hausner ends his horrible litany of gassings, children ripped apart, people burned alive, and cannibalism, which was as useful as it was biased. Automatically—because his words were spoken here— half the world will now think that Eichmann was responsible for all of this. This can only lead to disappointment later. But if this trial ends in disillusionment, all hell will break loose. The entire blame for almost everything is now more or less consciously laid on Eichmann's balding head. On the one hand, this is to satisfy Hausner's great zeal, in part based on the ignorance of someone who has never in his life seen an SS man in action. He arrived in Israel when he was twelve, in 1927. On the other hand, this is to satisfy the need for mankind to have a clear, simple, and horrible picture. It is no longer possible to believe in God; now let it at least be possible to believe in the Devil. But this procedure also discharges the other Nazis in an absolutely improper way. I am convinced that Hausner's approach meets with great approval in Germany. Hausner has announced that he will prove that Eichmann made the plan for the Final Solution, and that he was its organizer and executioner. I hope passionately that he will succeed—for if he does not, or not entirely (and Landau is not the kind of man to worry about the desire of the world: he administers justice in the Eichmann case), guilt will not be placed back where it belongs, but it will evaporate and disappear forever into nothingness. Hausner should have started small; then Eichmann's guilt could only have been greater than supposed, to the joy of everybody. The mechanism he has chosen now (out of pedagogical considerations, and compelled by advance publications in the world press forming one gigantic contempt of court) is irreversible.

When he finally sits down, he turns around and explores the room. But of course he is not looking for anyone: he wants to be seen. He is proud. It does not sit well with me although I usually draw pleasure from other people's vanity, too. The room should not be there, in his eyes. None of the three other prosecutors has ever looked out into the room, and neither has Servatius, Wechtenbruch, nor Eichmann himself. *We* are the ones looking. Mrs. Hausner is in the front row; she has not skipped a session yet.

After the adjournment, when Hausner's first witnesses are called, effectively beginning the presentation of proof, the House of the People is almost as full as on the first day. This does not last long. After some searching, a tall, blond man steps from the room into the witness stand, puts on a hat, and swears to God that he will speak the truth. What follows is not worth lying for. Police major Naphtali Bar Shalom is manager of Documentation of Office 06, and for hours he talks about archives, lists, catalogues, letters, and numbers. He makes a mistake—Landau corrects him. Landau makes a mistake—Bar Shalom corrects him. One after another leaves the room. Eichmann does not show any sign of being bored—but not of being interested either. The questions are now being asked by Public Prosecutor Gabriel Bach, also born in Germany. He looks like me, is the same age; he also lived in the Netherlands from 1938 to 1940, and he has the same kind of thumb. Twice already I have been asked for an interview.

In the afternoon, a more interesting witness appears, albeit with not such interesting information for the moment: Captain Avner Less, who interrogated Eichmann for almost a year. He appears in civilian clothes, as did Bar Shalom. I take him to be in his early forties. He has a tan, nearly bald head. From behind a pair of thick glasses, two blue eyes look frighteningly sharp into the world. Landau asks him whether the man he interrogated is present in the room at the moment, and Less points at the cage. I can barely suppress a laughing fit. To top the earlier absurdity, Landau tells the stenographer to record that Less confirmed that Eichmann is present in the room, which prompts the girl to nod somewhat offended, since Less did not say anything—he only pointed. What will become of stenography, she must be thinking. The remainder of the afternoon is spent on bibliophilic details.

In the evening, I talk with Wechtenbruch, Servatius's assistant, in the yard. When I ask him why he was not there in the afternoon, he says that he couldn't handle it anymore after Hausner's speech. Sitting next to a client who is, to say the least, a disgusting person and probably deserves the death penalty in any case, backed by a German government that boldly distances itself from them, and "with the sympathy only from the most unsympathetic," he could not deal with the murderous, head-on attack launched by Hausner. It is clear that he is starting to wonder whether participating in this case was such a good idea. But was it not going to be a fair trial? If not, they could have "beat[en]" Eichmann on "the back of his head with a cudgel right there in Argentina." I say that it does not give a fair impression when I see him sitting there, alone with Servatius, next to the four public prosecutors, who have the entire police machinery backing them up, the financial means of the entire state behind them, and the approval of the entire world; in addition, they have forty witnesses, and their state refuses to grant safe-conduct to witnesses for the defense. I try to trick him. With a smile I ask him whether the defense does not, for example, have other financial resources than this paltry couple of thousand dollars from Israel. His denial of my hinting at neo-Nazi organizations is not very convincing. If I had not seen them bothered by all sorts of small financial concerns, I would certainly not have believed him. Incidentally, he is going to Germany at the end of the week, "to shoot Nazis," as he calls it: to find witnesses. I get the impression it is not so much to get them here as it is to put Hausner in a dilemma. He speaks well of Hausner, by the way. Hausner approached Wechtenbruch spontaneously to say that Wechtenbruch can always come see him for documentation.

While we are having a glass of good whisky, he tells me about Eichmann's incredible memory for food. Even concerning his early SS dinners, in 1934, 1935, he can tell you exactly what soup they had, what meat, and whether the dessert was fruit or cake. But when asked about the deportation of Jews, he says: "One hundred and fifty or two hundred and fifty thousand, I do not recall the exact numbers. It has been too long." Then we go inside. The evenings turn chilly quickly in Jerusalem.

Wednesday, April 19. Less must have gotten a signal: today he appears in full uniform in the witness stand, with the obligatory rolled-up sleeves. The old fat court officer has finally replaced his blue battledress with a khaki summer uniform. Every day he positions himself near the door, five minutes before the official end of the session, uttering his savage cry on Landau's signal: "Beit Mishpat." I have been told this means "the court." When the time is exceeded, his squinting face darkens visibly. For the rest, he apparently has no contact with the words uttered, apart from the buzzer behind his head. When it buzzes, he jumps up from his chair and gets off in a quick, bumpy pace for Landau, to whom he has to go up two steps. Bets have already been placed as to when he will trip for the first time.

Furthermore, today we have finally amply heard Eichmann's voice, albeit not directly from his mouth. The visibility process is taking place in phases. The entire morning, Hausner played excerpts from Less's interrogation of Eichmann. When the session is adjourned until Friday, the room is split into three groups: those starting to doubt Eichmann's Genghis Khan guilt, those thinking he is lying, and those not thinking anything, but simply reporting what they hear.

The sound reproduction is bad, and from time to time even unintelligible. The military man who is tinkering with the controls, his face professionally contorted, has a blue Auschwitz number on the skin of his arm. Eichmann's strong Austrian accent is striking, but a certain Prussian curtness has taken away its melodiousness. The r is rolling, as was that of the Austrian Hitler and the Southern German Himmler. His voice is never raised: hesitant, looking for words, often starting anew, he fumbles ahead. Often he lapses into a hardly audible mumbling, sometimes changing to long silences. At such moments we are strangely sitting together: the judges, the journalists, the counsel, the prosecution, and Eichmann. Then we look at each other, and in the room the only thing that can be heard is the recorded chirping of the birds, which were singing around the former British police fortress near Haifa a year ago. At some point the sound of indifferent whistling approaches, and a door is slammed. A disgruntled Moshe Landau looks into the room, but he unexpectedly breaks into a smile and nods. It was a year ago.

Punctuated with a polite "Jawohl, Herr Hauptmann" and "Bitte, Herr Hauptmann," Eichmann tells Less that Heydrich told him, shortly after the war with Russia had broken out, that "the führer has ordered the physical extermination of the Jews." (The order to exterminate the Jews was never in any way put down in writing by Hitler: it inexplicably came out of nothingness to Göring. At any rate, Göring said it was a "führer's order" when he transmitted it to Heydrich; of course it was.) Eichmann says that at first he could hardly comprehend it and that he lost all interest in his work.

Shortly thereafter, at the Wannsee Conference, the matter was settled and agreed on definitively. Hausner, who went to the hairstylist today, says that he can prove that Eichmann was the big man on that infamous twentieth of January, 1942. Eichmann says that he had to be there in his capacity as transportation expert. Indicating who was to be gassed, whether there was to be gassing, whether they had to or could stop, whether it had to be increased, those were things he had (uttering quickly and softly) "never, never, never, never" been involved with, in spite of all the reports in the press. He gives the following authentic description of the conference itself, which resulted in millions of deaths: "I can remember that at some point someone or other took the floor, just as is customary—it was for the first time in my life that I participated in such a conference, the ones such high-ranking government officials participate in—but it happens in a very calm, very friendly, very courteous, very nice and sweet atmosphere, and not a lot is said; it also does not last long. A cognac is offered during the directives, and then the thing is over."

He says he never dared observe the gassings, and that is probably true. He did see everything before and after though: the stripping and the hair cutting beforehand, the pulling of the gold teeth and the removal of jewelry from anuses and genitals afterwards, and finally the cremation. While his voice is telling the story, he plays, with his eyes cast down, with the headphones in his hands. Such experiences left him in a dither for hours. This does not necessarily point to a large heart—especially not since he indicates that he was afraid to faint at the sight of the dying, as had happened to Himmler once, he claims. "When I see a gaping wound on someone today, then I cannot look. I belong to that class of human beings; people often tell me that I could not have become a doctor. I know even to this day how I would immediately visualize the thing in my mind, that I somehow agitating—a somehow agitating thing had happened, as occurs at times, so that one feels a slight shiver afterward, or so, as I would like to express it."

Less believable is the way he repeatedly cannot come up with the name of the poison gas. "With um . . ." (long silence; birds) "um . . . with um . . . what is it called . . . cyan—" Less: "Cyanide?" Eichmann: "Cyan-um . . ." Less: "Cyanide." Eichmann: "Cyanide or acid, as an acid it is called . . . um . . . cyanide acid . . ." Maybe some sort of "repression" is at work here, too; but, luckily, psychologists do not play any role in this trial.

Thus the entire morning is spent going back and forth over the reports of horrible events, which he thought were horrible, but of which he was at the same time a witness—and not a victim. Sometimes he tells about them in a horrible fashion, such as about the mass grave in Russia, from which a squirt of blood shot up.

Shortly before the collapse of Germany, he says, his colleagues in the Gestapo had false identity papers made, showing that they had been insurance agents during the war. But he refused. He would rather shoot himself than use a false document. Apparently this does not apply to a false document in the name of Ricardo Klement, with which one emigrates to Argentina. Yet, I would not conclude right away that he is "therefore" a pathetic liar. If man were that simple, we would be done quickly. I am also starting to view the infamous remark to his subordinate Wisliceny differently: that he would jump into his grave laughing, knowing that he was responsible for the death of five million Jews. The comparison with Satan is based to a large extent on this undoubtedly authentic phrase. But it must also have been bragging among friends. If some day the world press would make public what I have said to my friends, and especially what we have *laughed* about, mankind would also blanche.

This same human complexity, as much untruth as sincerity, must be seen in light of the statement he made to Less last year:

"My inner self has been prepared to make this general statement for a long time; only, I did not know in what direction fate would push me to make this statement. Already in January of this year (1960, so before his arrest), I was told that I would be tried this year. Precisely the same way I was told that I would not survive my fifty-sixth year. The first thing has already occurred, and the other is—I believe—inescapable. Just my knowing gives me a complete inner willingness to volunteer everything I know about me, totally disregarding my own person, which is not important to me at all anymore. My whole life I was used to being obedient, from the nursery until May 8, 1945. An obedience that developed in the years of membership in the SS into a cadaver obedience, into an unquestioning obedience. And what would disobedience have brought me? And who would have benefited from it? At no point in time, between 1935 and 1945, was I entitled to any involvement in planning, defining principles, or decision-making concerning the events during these ten years. For that, I was, in rank and service, in a much too subservient position. In spite of all that, I do of course know that I cannot wash my hands in innocence, because the fact that I was an absolute receiver of orders today certainly does not mean anything anymore today. Those who planned, made decisions, resolved, and gave orders have avoided their responsibilities cheaply, by committing suicide. Others belonging to this circle are either dead or not present. Although there is no blood sticking to my hands, I will certainly be found guilty of complicity in murder. No matter how that is, my inner self is willing to pay for the terrible events also personally, and I know that the death penalty is in store for me. I am not asking for mercy at all, because that is not due to me. Indeed, if it would mean a greater act of penance, as recent events have shown, I am willing to hang myself publicly, as a deterrent for everyone, for all the anti-Semites of the world's nations. Before that, let me write a book about the horror as a warning and deterrent for the youth of today and tomorrow, and then my life on Earth should end."

One can raise many objections here: that he shirks his responsibility on the one hand, and wants to play the martyr on the other. That he is willing to speak voluntarily *after* his arrest; that he rambles on about fate and apparently consults fortune-tellers; that he makes a distinction between those giving and those receiving orders, while these are married to each other, and are "one." Another question is how he would have spoken had Germany won the war. Would he have entered a monastery like the pilot of the Hiroshima plane (who also only carried out an order), or would he have been promoted to *Obergruppenführer*, deporting the Dutch people to Russia by now, as was Hitler's intention?

But it is nonsense to approach reality with hypotheticals. There is no SS General in the Kurfürstenstraße in Berlin, and none of the millions of others that would have done the same things as Eichmann, according to Wechtenbruch, are on trial. Germany lost the war and Eichmann is on trial: that is now final and irrevocable. But his tone is irrevocable too, heard through all the vagaries. In Nuremberg, General Field Marshall Keitel requested the honorable bullet instead of the humiliating noose. Still the military man, still lying. But the one who requests permission to hang himself publicly finds himself in the deepest pit of reality.

Thursday, April 20. Last night the Day of Independence began. Watched the fireworks over Jerusalem from the rooftop. Servatius was on the roof, too, with his bodyguard. In the other part of the city, in Jordan, the Arabs must have been gnashing their teeth.

Today off to the big parade, the one the Jordanians protested against in the UN. In the stands outside the city, with tens of thousands of people in the blazing sun. Most precious moment: when, in the presence of President Ben Zvi, his car came by empty, escorted by military with flying colors on galloping white horses. The president is a symbol, and that is why his empty car is a stronger symbol—and the white horses were snorting in the sun of Jerusalem, and that snorting silenced the rattling of the death train and the howling of the crematoriums—tears filled my eyes. What a great people! What a great history!

Truly, the most precious moment: when Prime Minister Ben Gurion arrived, escorted by motorcycles, and the last car of the parade was a taxi cab with a family that had ended up in the parade due to some traffic-related error and could not escape through the rows of people. The applause for the trembling family and the gray-faced driver drowned out that for the founder of the state.

After all, everything was done for that family! Here is the army, drilled by the British, waving with stretched arms, girls with automatic guns, berets over the eyes, here are the tanks rattling closer—may they finally have an army, please? And hardly any soldier looks "like a Jew." It could be the Egyptian, the French, or the Polish army. Not a trace will remain of the features of the Diaspora, just as in the days of Socialism not a trace of the proletarian was visible. The day will come when we will be allowed to say of the Jews that they did something filthy, such as massacring and razing an Arab village. Kfar Kassem for example—but not until that day has come will we speak of them as we do of other people who are good and bad, and not only one of the two: in short, as we speak of other people. And not until then will we ourselves no longer be anti-Semites or Semitophiles, but also like other people.

Friday, April 21. I don't know if anyone has ever looked at a trial as an artistic creation, as an object, as invisible as it is irrevocable, constructed by the judge, piece by piece, from the material gathered by the prosecution and the defense. Sometimes he refuses something; sometimes he asks for yet another thing; he tests, probes, brushes with a white hand over his mouth, reflects, considers the rules, applies the law, recalls verdicts, and slowly the object will grow. In a little glass house, there is a man he hardly looks at, whom he hardly thinks about—he looks over documents, stares at the ceiling, compares opinions, assigns numbers. When it is done, the man in the little house will fall over or remain upright. Even during the driest sessions I feel this fantastic, merciless process in progress.

Again, the entire morning was dedicated to playing the taped conversations with Less. I quit listening: a precious gift from the Israeli police has made it unnecessary. Six blue folios consisting of four thousand photocopies of typed pages, the complete interrogations, from May 29 until December 29, 1960. Every alteration in the verbatim transcripts confirmed by Eichmann: the pages are filled with his initials: the first days marked by a more or less clear *ei* or *eic*, which changes slowly into a vicious sign, something like a pointy *D*. In addition, every page has been initialed separately, also by Less, while Eichmann affirms with his signature, at the end of the transcription of each audio tape, that he has personally corrected the text. I will often return to this. The material I am interested in is all in here. The further trial proceedings will probably not add much.

Now I prefer to *look at* Less and Eichmann. From people close to the prosecution I hear that Eichmann fell physically ill when Less did not show up one day. Even if you are not Catholic or Freudian, you must feel the bond between the two men: Eichmann to the far left on the stage; Less to the far right. On a stage . . . I would indeed be very hard put to find a more dramatic scene. Two men—the one keeping the other prisoner; by chance one was not taken to the slaughterhouse by the other. Given this extremely intimate contact, they spent nine months in daily conversation, for hours on end. Then something is created that will naturally never be expressed in words—but they dream of each other, just as all of us here dream of Eichmann. During the day they try to catch one another, to outsmart one another, to melt each other's hearts, to be tough toward each other—but never will the one be without the other.

Now they meet again on stage, with a prosecutor and a judge between them. They knew it would come to this one day, but only now has the moment arrived. In Less there is shame; in Eichmann blame—no, not shame or blame: every now and then they look at each other. It is horrible.

Saturday, April 22. The road first leads toward Tel Aviv. On a hill in the distance is Samuel's tomb; the crusaders called it Mount Joie, mountain of joy, because from its top they first saw the Holy City. Soon the view is replaced by steep, wooded slopes on either side of the road. In 1948 the Arabs were here on both sides, and the shoulder of the road is littered with wrecks of provision trucks shot to pieces. Many received wreaths the day before yesterday. Lead paint protects them against rusting, for these are monuments for the younger generation: to remind them that the War of Independence did not consist only of victories.

At Lod Airport (biblical Lydda) the road bends to the north. We pass the birthplace of Jonah, and a little later we go through the sweet-smelling orange orchard of Samaria. As barren as the land is in the south, the more merciful it is here, barely sixty miles away. Descending from the Samaritan hills, we are welcomed by Jezreel Valley like an open hand. The hand lies open until the horizon, where the mountains of Galilee begin; at the thumb (if it is a left hand) it changes into the plain of Megiddo: Armageddon, where the last battle between the Suns of the Light and the Suns of the Darkness will be fought, for fighting has always taken place here: with the Midianites, with the Philistines, with the Pharaoh, with Vespasian, and with Saladin. Through a sea of wheat in the northwest we pass an odd molehill protruding out of the meadow a few hundred yards: Mount Tabor, on which Christ changed form for three of his disciples. Along the rocks, from which the first Christians threw themselves into the deep to escape their Roman persecutors, we climb into the mountains, and soon we reach Nazareth. A city with narrow alleys becomes visible against the slope; it is filled to the rim with Arab and American tourists. For a moment, jumping over the open sewers, one has the feeling of being in the Middle East; for the rest of the time this is Volendam.* The sacred places are filled with Leica pilgrims, and I will leave them for what they are (sacred); the Arab population is Catholic, by the way, but to irritate the Israelis it votes Communist, so that the city of the Son of God is the only one in Israel with a Communist majority on the city council.

Behind it we pass the village of Kfar Kana, where water was turned into wine, and we then go through the valley of Hittim, where in the twelfth century Saladin and his Saracens halted the Crusades: twenty thousand dead Knights of St. John and Templars, and a blood-holy dream.

The Sea of Galilee comes into sight a while later, indescrib-

---

*Volendam is a fishermen's village and tourist attraction five miles north of Amsterdam.

ably lovely. Warm and calm it lies in the deep, against the rugged mountains of Syria on the other side. On this motionless water the God walked, and the first thing I see, once we are down there, is a man on water-skis behind a motor boat. Again, I am the only one who begins to laugh, of course. In Tiberias I eat fried fish on the waterfront, half-naked, with a real *kaffia* on my head, which an Arab in Nazareth talked me into buying, and I imagine the fish is a man, as the Holy Scripture says, and I drink Carmelite wine.

Puffing, we drive along the lake upward, in the afternoon. We pass a village. What happened here? Mary Magdalene was born here. We pass a slightly rolling hill with a church on top. What happened here? It is the Mount of the Beatitudes. We arrive in the village of Kfar Nahum, "Village of Nahum," pronounced Kfarnahúm, also spelled Capernaum. My pious reader needs no more hints. Through the binoculars I see Arab fortifications in Syria, and a white UN flag.

Back to Tiberias, and farther southward along the water. We cross a sixty-foot wide river, in the shade of poplars, oleanders, and willows, whose tops almost touch each other: the River Jordan. It connects Lake Tiberias with its hellish counterpart: the Dead Sea. It is a country like a soul. If *any* country is holy, then this is it. There must be a reason for the fantastic, endless events that have taken place here for centuries—you can of course deny your belief in them, but not in the consequences. There *is* a church across from my house in Amsterdam. Twenty thousand knights *did* die in the Valley of Hittim. And I know the reason it all happened here, and not somewhere else: Israel itself is a human being. The loveliest lake on Earth is connected with the most horrible by a river in which the God was baptized. It is a human being. It is not geography, it is theography. I am not the only one who says that. There are others who agree with me. The Samaritan Gnostic Simon Magus for one, who is also mentioned by Luke in his Acts [of the Apostles] and much disputed by the Greek Fathers. Paradise is symbolic for the womb—an opinion already held, strangely enough, two thousand years before Freud. The river coming from Eden to irrigate the Garden embodies the umbilical cord. Galen claims that it is formed by four channels:

two for air and two for the blood. These are the senses of the nascent child. At the same time, this river is the Law that Moses gave. Genesis is the face, and Exodus the taste, for, Simon says, and here comes the theographical twist, when the child is born, the blood must wade through the *Red Sea.*

It is a thinking process I went through a long time ago. Mixed-up conceptions of a "psychological geography," Simon Magus-type attempts to design a globe of the "soul," all of which submerged in a flood. But when I write a story about a man who becomes petrified, then I still know that that can *only* take place on New Guinea, and when I write about a boy who does not stop growing, then that is *only* possible in Mexico. I do not have to stop and think about that. If a writer were to have a man petrified in Mexico or a boy grow on New Guinea, then I would laugh at him straight in the face: such an untalented, thick-headed storyteller.

By the way, we are still going around the lake, now across from Tiberias, on the narrow Israeli strip along the water. Gutted bunkers, trees shot dead. In the fighters' kibbutz Ein Gev, not far from where Jacob fought with the angel, we are watching the sun set, with the Syrians one hundred yards behind us. It is no different from the picture in the catechism. Oh, if only the Christians were not there!

Sunday, April 23. Since Eichmann is getting too close to me (he is also two seas, connected by a river in which the God is baptized), I quote SS-Obersturmbannführer Rudolf Höss, under whose command two million Jews were gassed in Auschwitz between 1941 and 1943. Even this unimaginable brute and dedicated family man, about whom I will report more later, got the shivers when speaking with Eichmann. In 1947 he wrote in his Polish cell, where he was awaiting the gallows: "I tried in every way to discover Eichmann's innermost and real convictions about this 'solution.' Yes, every way. Yet even when we were quite alone together and the drink had been flowing freely so that he was in his most expansive mood, he showed that he was completely obsessed with the idea of destroying every single Jew that he could lay his hands on. Without pity and in cold blood we must complete this extermination as rapidly as possible. Any compromise, even the slightest, we would have to pay for bitterly at a later date. In the face of such grim determination I was forced to bury all my human considerations as deeply as possible. Indeed, I must freely confess that after these conversations with Eichmann I almost came to regard such emotions as a betrayal of the führer. There was no escape for me from this dilemma. I had to go on with this process of extermination. I had to continue this mass murder and coldly to watch it, without regard for the doubts that were seething deep inside me."* I give up copying this boorish German. But it is enough. I just needed some antidote.

Monday, April 24. Witness Salo Wittmayer Baron, professor at Columbia University and a world expert on Jewish history, lectures under oath on Jewry. Very erudite, very long-winded, and with gestures of a professor, he tells the court all sorts of interesting things—but I fail to see the connection with Eichmann. Had the Jews been a cultureless tribe, for example something like the equally massacred Gypsies, would their deaths have been any less terrible? Is Eichmann on trial as a killer of people or as an annihilator of a culture? Is a murderer more guilty if a culture got lost in the process?

Over lunch with a small group of people, I ask Public Prosecutor Hausner this question. He thinks so—I don't. I cannot bring myself to say that I think it is as understandable as it is irrelevant and unfair to write history on the face of one man, who must be tried and who will certainly die. That is inhumane yet in a different way. But I don't want to ruin the ambiance. Jokes are being told and the conversation turns to Attila and Genghis Khan. I tell Hausner that I think Eichmann must have felt proud to be compared by him to Genghis Khan. "Proud?" With his high-pitched, boyish voice Hausner repeats it. He stares aimlessly ahead, and is silent. Then he introduces the theme: what would have happened

---

*Translated by Constantine FitzGibbon, *Commandant of Auschwitz: The Autobiography of Rudolf Hoess* (London: Weidenfeld and Nicolson, 1959), p. 155.

if Napoleon had had Hitler's anti-Semitism. Since no emigration to England and America had taken place yet, no Jew would have remained. But, a Swedish gentleman says, he did not have the technological possibilities for the extermination. Certainly, certainly, responds an official of the State Department, but there were also fewer Jews. Over a Wiener Schnitzel we finally agree that Napoleon would no doubt have been able to exterminate all the Jews. Then we consider what would have happened if Rommel had succeeded in breaking through from North Africa to Palestine. Eichmann would have followed a day later, and not a Zionist would have remained.

Responding to a question from Servatius, witness Baron certifies in the afternoon (after another professorial digression and after being called to order by Landau) that anti-Semitism stems from "the hatred of the non-equals." So that is it! What a genius! "The hatred of the non-equals"—that Sartre never thought of that! Servatius is not satisfied and brings the translators to despair with a question about "irrational grounds" and "events beyond the personal that would transcend," and then he mentions Hegel and Spengler and "the spirit in history, which moves forward by necessity and without human intervention." It follows dialectically that they wanted to exterminate the Jewish people, and that the result is a thriving state of Israel. What does witness Baron think of this theory—the theory therefore that sees Eichmann as the actual founder of the state of Israel? There is giggling and incensed hissing in the courtroom, but I feel it was an excellent move. The Great Cesspool is opening up: the slush in which Eichmann and Rosenberg and all of them were thinking. But, unfortunately, Baron loses himself in authoritarian baloney, saying that it is not very clearly thought out (nobody claimed it was—on the contrary), and ends by quoting from one of his own books, adding that it has been translated into Italian too. —I do not have the feeling I should stay in this Beit Ha'am much longer.

Tuesday, April 25. Imagine someone has become, more or less against his will, the protagonist of the TV show *This Is Your Life*. There he is on stage, with a full house, and he is being watched by the entire world. One after another come all the people who played a role in his life. But what are they actually telling us about the hero of the program? No, they have never met him, no. And then they proceed to tell their experiences with ex-colleagues of the protagonist, or subordinates of ex-colleagues.

Witness Grynszpan says that he was kicked and chased away. But did Eichmann kick him or chase him away? He was a member of the organization that kicked him and chased him away—but is it permissible to suggest, just like that, in a courtroom of all places, that it was Eichmann? And what is witness Benno Cohen, who was once the leader of the German Zionists, doing here? He describes the slow destruction of the Jewish community in Berlin, the boycotts, the pogroms, the humiliations—but at that time Eichmann was a clerk in the library of the SD.

And by now I am starting to wonder whether they caught the wrong man. Eichmann found himself in the SS hierarchy at a mysterious lull in a floating equilibrium: exactly halfway between those who gave orders (Hitler, Himmler, Heydrich) and the *Unterscharführer*, who indeed killed with their own hands. His guilt is substantial, but the problem is that a trial is held to *prove* guilt, and not to malign the defendant. The very disputable pedagogical setup of this trial, as it is increasingly taking shape, becomes downright odious when Hausner adds tactical intentions: to discredit Eichmann by enumerating all the Nazi crimes in connection with his presence, lacking concrete proof. It would be the same if in the Westerling trial (which has never taken place in the Netherlands, but perhaps Sukarno will have him kidnapped one of these days, entitled to it by the precedent of Eichmann), they would add up the profits of the Dutch coffee plantation owners.

The course of the trial will have to show how all this fits in. In any case, it surprises me that Judge Landau has not put a halt to the many irrelevant points. It might come to the point that they can only convict Eichmann for the killing of the Jewish boy who stole peaches from his garden. I asked Hausner yesterday whether that story is true. He said he will prove it "with God's help." But murder does not carry the death penalty in Israel.

CHAPTER 5

Wednesday, April 26. One out of four journalists has already left; half of those remaining will leave this week. The last few days the press has not been allowed in the first rows anymore. Now they are taken up by sophisticatedly dressed ladies from Tel Aviv, who devour Eichmann with their eyes, whispering in each other's ears, smiling while looking into the courtroom, waving to acquaintances in the balcony. Eichmann is becoming a society event for Israel's upper class. I leave the room—not because I am indignant, but because I realize the game is up. I return my headphones and try to book a seat on the next flight to Amsterdam. Since everything is booked full with journalists until Monday, I go to gather my belongings and take a *sherut* taxi to Beersheba, leaving Jerusalem behind; no regrets.

The *sherut* is an organization that arranges passengers so that cabs fill up. Thus the trip of over one hundred kilometers costs only three pounds (five guilders). For two hours we rattle in the gigantic Dodge, from the mountains down to the biblical city in the desert. Slowly it is getting warmer, and I do not have to think about the Bible anymore like three weeks ago, on the way to Sodom. At the terminal everybody gets out but me: I use the taxi to find a hotel. Unexpectedly, this half hour costs eight pounds—and it is all for naught: everything is booked full. I end up in a kind of homeless shelter, in an unlit back alley. Not bad for someone who had to go and observe the Bedouin. There are seven narrow beds in a stone room, less than two feet apart. On one there is a torn soldier's jacket, apparently not belonging to a soldier; on another a red piece of cloth, possessions tied in; a third bed has a cane or staff to mark it is taken. I put my luggage on my bed, offer a quick prayer to all the gods in this country, and hurry into the city.

The streets consist of yellow and shifting desert sand. The low houses to the left and right are made of dried mud, and they alternate with ruins of Arab houses and empty spots with stacked barrels or parked, gigantic trucks. But everywhere people are sitting on the street, and the main road is even asphalted. Jostling at the movie theater: this week *The Ten Commandments*. Place of action: around the corner.

At a small table on the street I eat *hummus*, a spicy Arab dip, followed by a gigantic mixed grill on a sixteen-inch plate—and slowly I am reconciled with the world. Around me are dust-covered, extremely sunburned soldiers straight from the desert, their automatic rifles over the backs of their chairs. Eichmann is receding; Jerusalem is receding, with its Orthodox Jews, Christian monks, and boiled chicken. This is how I like to eat, on the edge of barbarism. It makes me think of a meal years ago, high in the Alps, where the cows were grazing in the clouds. I was accompanying a friend who had to be there for a kidnapping case: a small child had disappeared, and the gnawed skeleton was found on the other side of the ravine. It could only have been an eagle. We had black bread and black sausage at the parents' home, in a cabin that had turned black due to the altitude.

The people are *more beautiful* too. In any case, that is what the fairytale-like dirty workers are that walk past: heroic desert proletariat, never Europeans, always North African immigrants. These are the Jews of Israel. In the army, they are the soldiers; the officers are Europeans. In cafés they are the waiters; the owners are Europeans. Later, in an artsy bar, the people become even more beautiful, and now I am starting to understand why all the hotels are full. On the barstool next to me is David Niven. Some sort of Italian-American super-cinerama coproduction in the Negev is being shot. As the evening wears on, the streets fill with the handsomest male material I have ever seen: all are being paid to moan and fall off galloping horses.

But I am worried about my suitcase, and when I enter the room, I am greeted by the snoring, tossing, moaning, and teeth grinding of six unknown people. When I finally fall asleep, shuddering, I dream that all are reading *Mein Kampf*, and then I show the trial to my girlfriend far away—and we are alone with Landau, Hausner, and Servatius, and in the courtroom we see Eichmann on TV, for he is in his glass cage in the audience.

Thursday, April 27. The Bedouin are in town. Today is their market day, and they are everywhere, in all the streets, in all the stores. I have breakfast in an outdoor café. Meanwhile I try to figure out what makes the Bedouin's presence in the city seem to be so curiously *light*. It is not their clothing. Except for the headscarves, often tied around their chins, they wear wide white pants, covered by thick, high-necked, ankle-long shirts, and jacket-like three-quarter-length coats, with a wide piece of cloth over their shoulders. In between they are covered with baldrics, crossways cartridge clips, and belts with silver daggers. Sometimes everything is new and made of beautifully woven material, but most often it all hangs down in indescribable rags. A few lower-ranked sheiks only wear a simple blue, ankle-length shirt with a belt around the waist.

Although I am distracted by two Dutch ladies behind me, one of whom is telling the other about a house in Ermelo* where the heating is installed along the baseboards, I figure out the lightness of the Bedouin: they are never in groups. Never will you find more than two together. Mostly they are alone, moving with strangely quick, flapping steps. With every step they raise their feet higher than we do, as though they are stepping over stones. Maybe it is a habit from the desert, or perhaps it is due to their colossal shoes. Everywhere they are on the shoeshiners' platforms, trying to get the worst dirt off using a knife. When two acquaintances meet, they put their hands into the other's, say very little, and move on. The position of their wide, low tents in the desert also shows this aversion to grouping: never are there more than five of them together, and even then they are one hundred yards apart, with the entrances facing away from each other. How different from Ermelo!

Near their market place, the first women are sitting in the dust underneath the bushes, or they are buying a roll of candy. When they put one in their mouths, I see that their chins and cheeks are lightly tattooed. Furthermore, the mouths are invisible and in front of their faces they have clinking coin chains. Girls eligible for marriage keep their head scarves over their faces, in such a way that only a minuscule hole remains, allowing one eye to peer through. As living poles, with only a tan hand visible, they

*Small town in the Netherlands.

shuffle through the sand in a row. One time I see a Bedouin girl, about nineteen years old, with her head and face uncovered. When I get closer, I see that she is crazy. She is laughing and begging. Local punks are poking fun at her, but it is the fact that she is unveiled that startles me.

The market itself resembles something out of the Old Testament. The shouting of the merchants can hardly be distinguished from the bleating and braying and yammering of the donkeys, the camels, and the black goats. Paws are inspected, hands are clapped, cattle driven back and forth, prodded with sticks. It is 95 degrees and I have my jacket over my arm. A Bedouin approaches me to exchange it for a lamb.

In the hills around the city, there are also Bedouin everywhere. There is one walking here, there are two sitting there; one is standing over there; another one is riding a donkey. It is as though a movie director has distributed them, with a great sense for harmony, but it is their own instinctive feeling for space that makes them take possession of the landscape, in such a light way, without conquering it, without destroying it, despised by a people that should be able to remember that one ought not despise peaceful minorities. Ruins of Arab houses line the road, destroyed in the war of 1948. Farther down, where the brown-yellow hills of the Negev begin, a high-power installation stands as a surreal dream of the camels. On the road along the market, diesel trucks rattle into the desert, like moving factories with smoking chimneys, leaving greasy dust clouds behind.

This gives me an idea: I have another three days left, and I am not attached to this bed. One hour later I am in a *sherut*, and I, too, disappear into the Negev.

After about thirty miles even the Bedouin think this is going too far. Nothing is left but the hilly yellow desert, with the pounding sun, and rocks that are jumping into heaps out of fear. Hour after hour we jolt along in our taxi, due south, to the end of Israel. For the Jews, apparently nothing can go too far. Every hour there is a kibbutz: some little white houses, a water tank on a hill, two paltry bushes and a gas pump. It is their intention to develop the entire Negev. The single-lane asphalt road is in and of itself a heroic achievement. Even when the terrain does not require it, the road meanders to render air strikes more difficult. Mostly the terrain does require meandering. A desert is not an endless stretch of North Sea beach, as I used to think in my youth, but it is rough in shape. Just when I think I have understood that, the taxi appears on the ridge of the Maktesh Ramon Crater, and for a few seconds I cannot breathe. From one end of the horizon into the other, an incredible bowl of 350 square kilometers lies at our feet: a nonhuman, motionless panorama of stone, which is coming toward us in silence. The road swerves down in hairpin bends, into the crater, then cuts through it in a straight line, as though the architect forgot all the strategy here and wanted to get out as quickly as possible. The desert suddenly turns to black, and later to pink, and also to sea green. Meandering wadis give the impression of fertility, from afar, but once we are driving through them, the bushes are several feet apart and the soil is drier than any spot in the Netherlands. I am having trouble with a Swiss idiot next to me, who points to everything he sees. When he sees a vulture, he points to it and says: "Bird." When he sees an antelope, he says: "Animal." When he sees a jackal, he says: "A dog."

After four hours we reach the oasis Yotvata, rich with palm trees. Another hour into the desert, I sit upright in the taxi: after all that stone, the Red Sea, so blue and so watery, lies ahead of us. The sun has just set and the landscape changes by the second. There are golden brown mountains to the left of the bay: Trans Jordan. The colossal violet mountains behind them: Saudi Arabia. The black mountains that cut through the bright sky to the right of the bay: Egypt.

Friday, April 28. On the border of Asia and Africa lies the port village of Eilat: a settlement of six thousand people on a coastal strip of seven miles, strategically as indispensable as it is vulnerable. In 1948 the strip of desert was conquered, without looking at the losses, by a section of the Jeep cavalry. Since it only rains once or twice a year for a couple of minutes, water is supplied via pipes from the sources of the Yotvata. Reversely, the oil from the Persian tankers is pumped up throughout the entire Negev all the way to Haifa in the north. The soil is brackish and stone dead. There is a "garden," in which dozens of gray trees and bushes are being kept alive through endless patience. A half hour after they have been watered, the cracks in the ground are back again, and big enough to park one's bike in.

But what one sees in April is a bay straight from the *Arabian Nights*. Five miles away, the little white houses of Akaba in Jordan lie at the foot of the mountains. Between Arabia and Egypt, I am the sole bather on a deserted beach. The whole day a dolphin as big as me has been tumbling ten yards away from me, always in the same spot. High up in the air, a flock of a thousand storks has apparently lost its way. A couple of times they try to cross the desert, but they return. Then they disappear over the tops of the Sinai, but after an hour they are back over the water.

Then I go in a glass-bottom boat to the coral reefs. Everything can be seen very clearly down to a turquoise depth of thirty feet. The reefs are cauliflowers and brains and livers as big as rooms, filled with red and green caves. Fish with extraterrestrial colors swim through them: fish with eyes on their backs, fish with two tails, fish with antennae, fish with legs, fish with mustaches, fish with canes, and fish with hats on; there are also fish like snakes with crocodile snouts, fish like yards of adhesive tape, and fish like nothing more.

Saturday, April 29. Since it is the Sabbath and every action is strictly forbidden, I have the heathens working for me, and I am copying some opinions from Israel's enemies about the Eichmann trial.

In Jordan, K. S. Khatchadurian asks how justice can be done by the killers of Count Bernadotte and of many Arab women and children from Kfar Kassem, Deir Yassin, and Kibya. Reporters will never be objective, for how many can run the risk of losing advertisements from Jewish and Zionist businesses? "The world has ignored the crimes of the Zionists. We are asking it to stand up as one, to bring this farce to an end, to force the Zionists to obey the UN resolutions, and to allow the Arabs to return to their land, their houses and property." In another article: "The Zionists themselves are on trial here. Will they leave this man alone and allow him to return to his family and his country, as a sign of respect and gratitude for what the UN has done for them, and for what the Germans have given in payments—or will they hang him?"

In the Egyptian weekly *Akher Sa'a*, Mohamed al-Tabi'I writes about "the disgusting historical lie, spread by the American press, that the Nazis killed six million European Jews. The trial against Nazi officer Adolf Eichmann is based on this lie."

The magazine *Al-Difaa* explains why Eichmann is in a glass cage. This is not to protect him from bullets, but to enable them to turn off the microphone, should he start saying things the Zionists do not like. —It is a bit clumsy then of the Zionists that they left the cage open on the side turned away from the room.

While I am writing this on my private balcony, in the distance lies Akaba on the edge of the sea like a piece of starry sky fallen down. In the middle of the dark, motionless bay, a lighted ship comes to anchor. The moon is over Arabia. In the darkness below, I see the hotel manager on a bench. I imagine my love has been killed in Europe, and my friends too, and that I will not go back. That is the situation of that man in the dark down there. At the same time, the beauty around me is transformed into a face, only distorted in yet a different way, one of nonhuman reality, accessible only through death.

6

$$\boxed{5/21/61}$$

A Ruin in Berlin

Back from the summer into the spring. In rainy Amsterdam, I am reading the blue books from the Israeli police, while in Jerusalem the examination of the witnesses is getting underway.

On July 6, 1960, at around half past two, Captain Avner Less asks Eichmann how many floors his office in Berlin had. In line with his character, the prisoner immediately gives an accurate description of the entire building, including the location of the restrooms; he even draws a map, which was not reproduced. The intention of Less's question will only become clear later. Since many of the offices and rooms were always empty, a certain Paul Blobel was billeted with him in 1945. This *SS-Standartenführer*, hanged in 1951, an architect and alcoholic from Düsseldorf, was initially the leader of Einsatzgruppe [death squad] 4A in Russia, in which capacity he once established the record of 33,771 executions in two days. That was in the winter. In the spring he drove past the ravine Babi Yar, near Kiev, with a Gestapo agent for religious matters. There the visitor noticed, to his surprise, small explosions everywhere in the ground, which threw up small piles of dirt. "This is where my Jews lie buried," said Blobel. The thaw setting in released the gasses from tens of thousands of corpses. Later Heydrich, who found him to be too softhearted and advised him to pursue a career in the porcelain business, appointed him leader of Kommando 1005, the so-called *Exhumierungskom-mando*, "exhumation unit." In that capacity he had to open the many mass graves in Poland and Russia and efface all traces, which he tried to do, in vain, with petroleum, dynamite, and bone grinders. According to Wisliceny, this party member was a good friend of Eichmann's, who is said to have put him in charge of designing the first gas chamber in 1941. Eichmann denies this. Blobel belonged to a different department, so there was no direct official connection between them—this is contradicted by a note from Höss, who mentions "Blobel from the Eichmann department." With the point about the billeting, Less is trying to corner Eichmann now (somewhat against the instruction to abstain from cross-examining him). Why did Blobel come to him in the Kurfürstenstraße? Why not to the Gestapo headquarters in the Prinz Albrechtstraße? Because it was overcrowded there already, says Eichmann. In addition, Blobel came to live in the building next to his, but he never even saw him.

What fascinates me most in this relatively insignificant passage is not the truth. It is the geographical complexity. A man is kidnapped from Buenos Aires. Two months later, in Haifa, he describes a building in Berlin. I am reading about it in Amsterdam, while he himself is in Jerusalem, listening to a story told by someone from Warsaw while he was, let's say, in Paris at the time. It is difficult to find the words to express what I mean. To Germans "movement" has always meant more than it does to others. It is not only "necessary relocation," but it also opens up fresh sources of the soul. German movement is mystical and dangerous. The *Wandervögel* of yesteryear transformed under Hitler into an entire marching people. Until 1939 they marched in Germany, all the time, day and night, through all the streets, woods, fields, and roads, in the Jungvolk, in the Hitlerjugend, in the Bund Deutscher Mädel, in the SA, in the SS, and in the army. Party philosopher Alfred Rosenberg officially called life a marching column, which is not interested in where it is marching, just that it is doing so. Starting in 1939, the movement broke through the German borders everywhere, and Göring's geographical lust is sticking out a mile when, in a speech on January 30, 1943, he talks about the front "from the Arctic Cape to Biscay, down to the African desert, and far to the East, on to the Volga," where Germany "is bleeding, but victorious." Eichmann hurries to Vienna, and to Prague, and to Paris, and to Lublin, and to The Hague, and to Budapest . . . and when the movement finally peters out in its own distances, and the entire world, in turn is moving toward Berlin, the movement continues through Eichmann, in a deadly silence: Austria, Germany, Switzerland, Italy, Argentina, and finally Israel. By then the other Germans have been moving in Volkswagens through Europe for a long time, in yellow sandals and with white hats—"from the Arctic Cape to Biscay, down to the African desert."

I cannot verbalize what I want to say. I put the transcribed interrogations in my bag, and fly to Berlin.

WILHELMSTRAßE 102. Not checked by the Volkspolizei, I walk through the Brandenburg Gate, from which an empty Unter den Linden stretches out. Past the show palace of the Soviet legation, I turn right, into the deserted Wilhelmstraße. The difference with five years ago, when I was here before, is the increased cleanliness and the increased silence. The extermination of the world was once coordinated from this street. Excited masses surged through the night, awaiting the news of a victory. Generals crawled out of cars and disappeared into the colossal buildings. Now nobody was anywhere to be seen. In the clear sky above the space that is swept clean a sudden shimmering begins, which intensifies all the colors. The spot where the Reich's Chancellery once stood has changed from a field of stubble into a well-trimmed, bright green lawn. They have succeeded in blowing up the toppled, gigantic, concrete egg, the air shaft of Hitler's bunker. A grass bump, just as gigantic, now indicates the spot where the cockroach was exterminated. The remainder of the palace next to it, Ribbentrop's State Department, has apparently just been razed: there is a baroque pile of rubble, from which bent iron beams are sticking out like the legs of a horrible insect. I stop to listen to the silence. In the distance someone is practicing tuba. On the other side, with a large lawn in front, is the spared Propaganda Ministry of Göbbels, now East Germany's Ministry of Culture. An old man is sweeping the sidewalk. There is not another living soul around. It is the silence of the past. Something happened here; something was decided; and nothing is left. There are not even ex-Nazis staring wistfully at the green bump—I am the only one here. Not out of wistfulness, but because I want to understand something: how something can change. But it is becoming increasingly less clear, and I do not understand anything. The houses in the distance are decorated with red posters, which only I am reading: PEACE WILL CONQUER WAR. WEST BERLIN: NOT A POWDER KEG BUT A FREE CITY. ARTISTS AND CULTURE PROVIDERS, INSPIRE THE WORKERS WITH YOUR ART FOR THE VICTORY OF SOCIALISM.

A little later I cross the border again, but now I am checked. The Vopo examining my pass has a dirty look on his face, but then he salutes me, happy to see I am Dutch. Fifty yards farther, after an exchange of head shaking with the West Berlin police, I am in front of a large field of weeds and low rubble. Aided by a 1927 *Griebens Reiseführer*, the most deceitful book I possess, I locate the spot where Wilhemstraße 102 used to be, the former palace of Prince Albrecht, later of Reynhard Heydrich, opposite the Kochstraße. Thistles. It is here that Eichmann started his career in 1934, as a clerk in cataloging at the Central Office of the SD. The interrogations have shown, meanwhile, that the whole thing was just due to a misunderstanding. When he was tired of military life in the new concentration camp Dachau, and he applied for the Sicherheitsdienst des Reichsführers, he assumed that that was the bodyguard of Himmler; that he would stand, as he had seen in the illustrated magazines, on the running board of cars, drive around a lot, and see something of the world. To his dismay he became an office clerk, and he did not realize his mistake until a few days later.

Set somewhat to the back, in no-man's-land, in the Niederkirchnerstraße, once the Prinz Albrechtstraße, lie the remainders of the former Gestapo headquarters, which used to be a school for industrial art. The entire building collapsed into the basement, in which thousands had been tortured to death, from the unknown teacher to the Wehrmacht generals and high-ranking SA leaders on the "Night of the Long Knives."

(A few days later, back in Amsterdam, on Pentecost morning I am awoken by a phone call from The Hague: a lady showers me for minutes, in the Dutch of the higher walks of life, with compliments for my Eichmann articles, which distinguish themselves so favorably by their human tone and their lack of hatred. When I finally discover an opening in the deluge, I ask if there is maybe a second reason why she is calling me up this early in the morning. She hesitates. Yes, no, that is to say, yes, she and her husband are also working on certain historical studies, no, not published yet, the time is not ripe for it, but perhaps I . . . because exactly thanks to the tone of my articles . . . I tell her to send me something. No, that is . . . I must understand . . . she and her husband would prefer to get to know me personally first. No, she prefers not to give her name for now, but maybe we can meet somewhere . . . feel each other out . . . Not much later, I hang up. I know who called me; at least, I have no other explanation. Nazis. Somewhat baffled I go back to sleep, and I have the following dream. With giant jumps I am hovering through the Wilhelmstraße, in the direction of the Brandenburg Gate, accompanied by the rhythmic clapping of some of my friends, who are standing on the corner of the Kochstraße and following me with their eyes. At the height of the Göbbels Ministry I come to a standstill. Just as I try to hover back, which is difficult due to the strong headwind, a light grey ball rolls through the gutter. I look up to see who threw it, and in the distance, near the Brandenburg Gate, I see Eichmann approaching. He is looking at me, and I look at the ball at my feet. I cannot make myself throw the ball back. I squat and wait. My friends have also fallen silent. When Eichmann picks up the ball and returns, without saying a word, I say: "I am sorry I did not throw back the ball." For a moment he looks around, silently, and then he walks on. At that moment I hear a woman behind me say: "My husband and I think that is great: at his age, still so quick, and so handsome.")

AM GROSSEN WANNSEE 56–58. The S-Bahn leaves the city westward and then goes through green spring woods for about twenty minutes. Unexpectedly the lake is sliding into view. Sailboats lie slanted in the water. Treetops are basking in the sun. Dressed pleasure boats fill with day trippers on the quay. The spot where Heinrich von Kleist and his girlfriend committed suicide is close to the station. I tell a cab driver my address, and after five minutes we turn off the main road into a quiet side road, which is almost roofed over by foliage, and which leads, curving nicely, to the Heckeshorn peninsula.

At an impressive cast iron gate I ring the bell. *Schullandheim* it says on the sign. At the end of a driveway bordered by pine trees, some slender, white pillars are visible, and a door that is open; the remainder of the building is hidden behind the trees. When a female voice through a small loudspeaker asks who I am, I simply say I am from Amsterdam. For some reason the gate buzzes open. With every step I take, the elegant, pavilion-like eighteenth-century castle becomes more visible. Any moment now Goethe can step out, accompanied by the duke of Weimar, talking about the "primeval plants." At the door, the housekeeper apologizes for the fact that the headmistress is on vacation.

I am being told everything about the *Schullandheim*, but don't get any farther than the shiny, polished parquet floor. While she is explaining that children from all over the country, and even from abroad, from the Netherlands too, spend a few weeks here in a class with their teachers, and that they are taught over there, in that room, and that they dine in that room, and play games in that room, I peek through the open garden doors to the terrace, to the marble vase on the lawn, to the trees and the lake in between, where one can see sailboats, and where the pleasure boats sail past with music.

Two slender Corinthian pillars support the ceiling. The doors are inlaid with mosaics from Pompeii. Eichmann sent out the invitations. On January 20, 1942, on this parquet, Heydrich announced to the highest authorities involved, with a glass of cognac in his hand, that the führer had decided on the "Final Solution to the Jewish Question." Everyone understood immediately what was meant by that, although nobody could grasp it right away. Eichmann had prepared Heydrich's speech; he was the twelfth on the protocol.

"Nothing is better for children than a change in environment," says the housekeeper. "They love it here."

KURFÜRSTENSTRASSE 116. It is still there. As a continuation of the shiny Kurfürstendamm with its heated, candy-like outdoor cafés, behind the ruin of the Gedächtniskirche, at the level of the new Hilton Hotel, a dark colossus stands in the middle of a deserted prairie. When this area was destroyed in November 1943, it escaped the worst hits. Its pompous sandstone outside wall is even practically unscathed. The tall windows are all blinded. In front of the many windows of number 115, which forms an architectonic unity with it, laundry is hanging out to dry. A bunch of impoverished children are playing on the porch. Now this building, in which Blobel allegedly lived, is a shelter for refugees from East Berlin.

Number 116 looks out, blinded and stony, over the deserted plain. While I am memorizing this, I have to think of Eichmann's face in Jerusalem. This resembles it. The rattling of the death trains has died out across Europe, the shrieking in the subterranean gas chambers has been absorbed by the earth, the ashes have been washed by the Weichsel [Vistula] to the sea. A sign over the gate to the inner court reads:

> ACCESS FORBIDDEN
> FOR UNAUTHORIZED PEOPLE
> MORTAL DANGER

The backside of the building has been considerably damaged. Walls are destroyed, and the roof has been knocked off. When Eichmann returned from Budapest in January 1945, where he had arranged the deportation of hundreds of thousands, "business-like work," was no longer possible, he told Less on June 1, 1960. It was chaotic; they were bombed every night, and the Russians were approaching Berlin from all sides. He decided to fight to the bitter end and to turn his office into a fortress. For years he had been building a subterranean system of bunkers. Now he set up machine-gun nests in the basement and also in the surrounding ruins. He had the tram rails broken up and he made tank barricades from them. He also had bigger artillery put in, and provisions. While his colleagues had false ID papers made for themselves with the names of insurance agents, he says that he was looking forward "to the fight for Berlin, for I knew my cleverly built defense system, and for me there was no other thought in the world than now in this final fight for Berlin to encounter death—if I could not find it like that, at least I should look for it."

But to his dismay he was sent away by Himmler on a new mission. He was to put a few hundred prominent Jews from the concentration camp in Theresienstadt somewhere for safe-keeping: the insane, idiotic *Reichsführer* thought he could use them as hostages during his intended negotiations with General Eisenhower. Eichmann went on his way: "Once more, with pain in my heart, I had to leave behind my position for defense, which I had already arranged—and I did not know if I could still use it, for the front was advancing with giant leaps toward Berlin." He was right. No matter how he hurried to be back on time, he found the way to Berlin cut off. If only he had died en route, he sighed to Less: "In Berlin I could not fight anymore either. I had always prepared everything everywhere, and planned everything everywhere, but I never, never got to apply it; in my personal life things went just exactly the way they went all those years with my professional involvement in whatever site of land and soil for the Jews. I do not know, my life was bewitched or something. Whatever I planned, and whatever I wanted, whatever I did, and whatever I wanted to do, Fate somehow stopped me and Fate thwarted my plans. It does not matter what it was. Captain, you have heard my description: it is the same down the line."

Over the main entrance a red sign reads BRÜDER-VEREINS-HAUS. That is what it was before the SS moved in: a Jewish club-house, which was changed into the Zentralstelle für jüdische Auswanderung [the Central Office for Jewish Emigration]. After the expulsion and destruction, respectively, of German Jewry, Eichmann's Gestapo-Amt IV B4 kept its offices there. In Vienna and Prague he later followed the same system, by nestling exactly in the center of Jewish life—like a cancer.

Since the gate is closed, I go to find out more in the local pub, which is situated in a corner of the building. The disaffected owner refers me to Frau So-and-So, who has the key.

In a side street of the Kurfürstendamm I find her (having waited for her for two hours) behind a front wall that is pockmarked by bullets and bomb shells. In a musty office, with a second old lady behind a dilapidated typewriter, she speaks to me. No, it will not happen. She once admitted a journalist, who then wrote nothing but sensationalistic nonsense: he described the gate of the coal shed as "Gestapo bars in front of the torture chamber"; by the way, her salary does not allow her also to show foreigners around. I tell her I am immensely rich and would love to leave a contribution toward a new typewriter on the table; that I am not a journalist, but a criminologist wanting to compare Eichmann's description of the house to the actual house, in order to test the reliability of his memory—but no matter how I beg, flatter, threaten, and feign, a little later I am back in a taxi, with in my head nothing more than the name of the tabloid.

Maybe they can help me there. There is nobody at the editorial office anymore; after a lot of rummaging I finally find the article in question, aided by the porter. An editor I call tells me in a surly tone who wrote the article. The man got a transfer to Frankfurt two weeks ago. Luckily he gives the name of another paper, which also ran an article about the house, albeit later. The paper has its offices in the same building; I take the elevator up and find myself in the chaos of a morning paper. Forty-five minutes later I know exactly who wrote the article in that paper. The man was operated on for kidney stones yesterday.

Back in the Kurfürstenstraße, I memorize the house inch by inch. We shall see who is the strongest. Underneath the eave I suddenly see a window with closed curtains. In the courtyard I discover the entrance, and I jump up the six flights of stairs. A skinny woman of about fifty, in a coat and with a hat on, opens the door. When she learns I am interested in the house, she showers me with insults. I must be a journalist! The other day someone wrote about her too—can she help it that she is poor and that she has to live here? Why don't they give her a decent dwelling! After fifteen minutes I am walking with her through the vast attics, and then over what is now the roof, but what used to be tiled kitchens. In a built-up shaft, a dark stairway leads to the inside of the building; in front of it is an immovable, padlocked iron gate. We try ten keys, but none fit.

But now I have a new address: that of a lady whose deceased husband was the doorkeeper of Kurfürstenstraße 116, at the time of the Brüder-Verein as well as during Eichmann and for a couple of years more after the war, when the building was called Thefi-Haus and when it was the entertainment center of the neighborhood.

The old widow does not dare let me in.

"I am seventy-two and have trouble walking, you must understand . . . I cannot tell you anything, I am sorry. Herr Eichmann was never unpleasant to me. He was often away. You never knew whether he was still there or not. If he did not say 'Heil Hitler,' then I did not either. One of the others, Herr Günther, once said to me: 'Do you know that he is a lieutenant colonel?' Then I said: 'I am a human being too.' That Herr Günther, when he looked at you, you had the feeling that his eyes went right through you. Herr Eichmann often had words with my husband, but he knew he could not get anyone in his place, so the next day he called him in to reconcile their differences. My husband was such a pighead: he accepted anything from the SS. 'Let them put me in a concentration camp,' he used to say."

"Did you know a certain Blobel?"

"Blobel? I don't know anymore. I think I have heard that name before. That must have been one of them. They were all the same. That he didn't shoot himself, Herr Eichmann, I don't understand. If I were to see him today, I would say to him: 'Herr Eichmann, you ought to be ashamed of yourself!'"

But she does not have any keys anymore, and, not knowing what else to do, I go back to the pub, and I try to work on the frightful owner with talk and booze. But her hair is dyed red and she is standing like a rock. I consider using force, and I look around to see if there is a nail with a key somewhere . . . Grinding my teeth I go outside again, and I take up a position on the other side. Never before was I so sure I was going to get in! I am sweating, thinking up evil tricks . . . and here, at this instant, I will unfortunately have to enshroud my report in darkness.

We will continue half an hour later: I am in the hall of the former Amt IV B4, Eichmann's headquarters.

With the interrogation in my hands I am staring, my mouth wide open, through the dark, deserted space. A chirping, cooing, and fluttering of wings is coming from all directions, but I cannot see any movement. Flanked by Doric columns, a wide staircase of soft pink marble is ascending, to the left and right I see dark rooms, stuffed with brooms, cases, and empty bottles. (". . . there was the registry, secret Reich registry—, secret registry, and open registry. Otherwise, in the whole front part of the building, nothing was left, except for downstairs the guard of course, downstairs, for the rest there was nothing left at all. And now one had to, when one went in here, in the front, then one entered in some sort of foyer, and from there a broad staircase went up . . .") Through the funereal silence, which the birds cannot break, I go up the stairs. I realize I am in an administrative haunted castle with no equals. The high walls are made of marble too. Through a kind of gate, over which the words BRÜDER-VEREIN are carved, I enter a hallway where the walls have been painted with depictions of funny scenes, such as an American soldier lifting up a girl's skirt, a girl behind a stroller, a peace angel clearing up rubble. Those were the days of the Thefi-Haus, when they danced with Americans, made love with them, and ate potato salad. Everywhere in the side rooms there are rotting bars and broken chairs. (". . . Moes was here once, and Woehr, and some other inspector, they had three rooms together . . .") The hallway runs into a rundown, round room, where the walls are covered with colorful pieces of paper and beer ads; cardboard advertising bottles are in the alcoves; there is a small podium, and straw is hanging from the soaked ceiling. (". . . people gathered in the evening in a round room, when they played music. There was, I believe, a, a, a piano in there, it was brought in at some point, by those in charge of the SS troops. Then there were violins and such things, they played music. For the rest there were no office rooms down there, no . . .") According to the story in the interrogation, which is fairly poorly organized, and which lacks Eichmann's drawing, there is a second room on the other side of this room, which has stairs going up to the backside of the building, where the actual offices of IV B4 were. The podium is probably of a later date and closes off the passage to those offices. I walk back and try to get to it from the other side. In the great hall, to which the stairs lead, two new sets of stairs go up even farther. (". . . broad stairway . . . which lost itself up here, once over here, a narrow hallway, and over here, a narrow hallway . . .") The left stairs are inaccessible because the steps are covered in ceiling rubble; the other leads to a cloak-room, whose hooks have not been used in some thirteen years. (" . . . but if it went up any more, that I can't . . . now . . . I believe . . . certainly . . .") There is no reason for him to hide it; he truly does not remember it anymore, since he always went upstairs via the round room. There certainly is a broad stairway there, now locked off by a small plywood wall, no doubt to keep post-war lovers out. A small door allows me to go upstairs, and there begins the great destruction. The sun is shining through the holes in the roof, and as quietly as I can I look at the sparrows, which are fluttering back and forth through a room as big as a country church. Grey pigeons glide whooshing into the windows and then walk cooing to their nests, which they have made among the inde-scribable chaos. All the woodwork is burned down, the floor is a grey plain of ashes, in which the iron crossbeams are visible; everything else is covered in rotten beams from the roof and bro-ken roof tiles. There is a zinc bathtub, which was probably in the attic. The scorched, soaked, and cracked walls were once covered with mirrors; plaster columns have half fallen off their iron skele-tons. (". . . a very large room, which was always empty . . .") The tabloid in my pocket has a picture of it. Its subtitle says that the desk of the mass murderer stood here, where with one stroke of the pen, he . . . But it was not here. Surrounded by fluttering birds,

I carefully walk through it, making sure to stay on the iron beams, as an authorized person, for now there is truly mortal danger. On the other side I enter a complex combination of blown away walls and half rooms. Concrete stairs, which I go up on, lead in a mysterious way in the open air, giving me an unexpected view of half of Berlin.

Supposing that these are the stairs he mentioned earlier, I go down completely on these, and indeed I hit a pitch dark room; its center is covered with a pile of rubble. (". . . at the same time there was a room here that was empty, here, a big room that was empty . . . Now up these narrow stairs here, backward it went up through the back side of the building, that was occupied by Günther and by me . . .") I go upstairs, but again I have trouble orienting myself, and I end up in the open sky. Through the big room I walk back, enter a room to the side (". . . some rooms for the people who did their service at the central office . . .") and now I suddenly notice three windows, in the addition on the other side, where I have just been. I overlooked an entire floor! Back to the backside I try to feel my way through the ruins with the help of my guidebook. (". . . There it went up, one set of stairs, through some doors, which had been installed in the course of time, and then one would enter a complex, which looked, let's say, about like this. Then here was the anteroom, that was my room . . .") There are no more doors, the existence of walls can often only be discerned by the different placement in the floor, or not at all. But I am about in the burned room with the three windows. I estimate it is about fifteen by twenty feet, so not especially big. Softly the wind blows in. When I hit the wall, kilograms of rotten plaster fall down. By the following passage, which goes, in an extremely complicated way, via the rooms of Günther and Novak, to the telephone switchboard and the restrooms, I try to settle the matter. Not far from where I end up, a lead water pipe is hanging from the wall. So was it Eichmann's room? Maybe it was Eichmann's room.

I feel the way Judge Moshe Landau must feel.

7

$\left(\ \text{5/28/61}\ \right)$

The Horror and Its Depiction

Only in times of the plague or during the invasion of the Huns have horror stories been told on such a scale as in the past few weeks. But never did people listen in such large numbers and directly via radio, newspapers, and TV to live reports from a freshly painted witness stand. Children were sent out of the room, newspapers were hidden, and many refused to read any more reports after the first day. The blow hit exactly as hard as Hausner had intended. Because the witnesses talked about past experiences, which will never truly be "past" because they will always remain present to them, as if happening today, and maybe even closer—that is why this "today" created itself for those who did listen. The things heard in the past few weeks happened only the moment the world heard them: in the spring of 1961.

But almost immediately there was a response: telling stories is not a free ride. Right after the first witness accounts, the numbing was noticeable. Not much later, say after the second week, the opinion could be heard that the Jews had better stop talking about their misery; we knew already. And of course it is unbearable for a citizen dealing with serious business problems, with a troublesome son, and with a death in the family to be confronted with a family whose father was gassed, whose child was torn to pieces, and whose mother was bitten to death by those dying in a mass grave. That is unbearable. The Jews should stop talking about it now. We know it already.

But that is exactly it: we will never know. It is not knowable. And resentment awakens within the listener who is confronted with the story that trivializes the seriousness of his own. But when resentment awakens where Jews are involved, it starts to smell like gas. Of course they know that in Israel too, but there they don't worry about it. I have seen their armies march. Whoever hurts a Jew, out of resentment perhaps, will be thrown a hand grenade; and the Jew who wants to stay out of Israel, well, he is at his own mercy.

This begs the question: to what extent is the depiction of horror the cause of horror?

Without a doubt Nazism originated more from certain imagery than from certain ideas. Without mentioning them as causal relations, we can at least establish that Nazism was *preceded* by numerous images, conveying its world. Art foreshadowed what was going to happen. We have no reason to forget that the world that has been conveyed at the foot of the Mount of Olives over the past few weeks shaped the more or less secret desire of preceding generations. What does that world of desire look like?

After the ninth circle of hell, Virgil and Dante left the inside of the Earth at a point diametrically opposite to Jerusalem. We are wandering across its surface, without a classical guide; and our mouths are not singing, and the circles are not called Cocytus or Ptolomea, but Treblinka, Belzec, Lviv, Minsk. For it wasn't even hell: it was a sacrificial place for the innocent . . . and God had fallen asleep; and some, who have held a mirror in front of God's mouth, claim that He died a long time ago.

Under dead light the world of the witnesses forever lies: children playing, assaulted on the streets by SS men, thrown into trucks, shoved by the thousands into freight trains, and transported to the gas chambers (*witness Peretz*). Sick children, thrown out of the children's ward on the fifth floor (*witness Ross*). Babies, ripped apart like a rag in front of their mothers' eyes (*witness Buzminsky*). Neighborhoods, chosen at random, closed off, starved, and then burned. The inhabitants, jumping out of their windows and attempting to crawl with their broken limbs; the soldiers, first laughing at them for a while, and then throwing them into the fire. Churches filled with believers set ablaze (*witness Masia*). Old priests forced to play horseback-riding matches on each others' backs (*photograph*). Old women made to scrub a square clean with toothbrushes (*photograph*). Orchestras playing dance music, while thousands of naked families are being executed (*witness Wells*). "An old woman with snow-white hair was holding the child in her arms while singing a song and tickling it. The child cooed with pleasure. The couple observed the scene with tears in their eyes. The father was holding a ten-year-old's hand, speaking to him softly. The boy was fighting back his tears. The father pointed to the sky, stroked his hair, and seemed to be explaining something. Then the SS man called" (*witness Gräbe*). Dogs being given sugar cubes for having bitten flesh out of a girl (*witness Buzminsky*). Mountains of corpses, mountains of shoes, mountains of glasses, mountains of artificial limbs, sheds filled with women's hair, buckets full of gold teeth. Meadows covered with skulls and bones (*witness Berman*). Naked people in winter, covered with water and frozen (*witness Neumann*). People killed by injection and boiled in big pots because their skeletons had to go to the museum. Others who ate from them. People who ate from already blackened corpses. Groups of men arriving in concentration camps in tuxedos, with top hats and walking sticks (*witness Wells*). A man who has to choose between his wife and his mother; if not, both will be executed (*witness Dworzecki*). Torturing and executions taking place in cellars in the middle of all cities. Gas chambers being so filled that the naked people had to hold their arms above their heads, above which the children were laid. A man who for two days is forced to look for his own body among hundreds of corpses, only to find his daughter, and then his father, and then his wife.

(The German under his glass dome listens motionless. Sometimes he bends over somewhat stiffly to take a note with his rheumatoid hands.)

This world, which has ruined the history of Europe forever, lies there as a threat. He who speaks of "the past" with a sigh of relief is wrong. The Europe of Raphael and Goethe is as much related to the Europe of today as a bucket of milk with the curdled crap that results from adding a splash of vinegar. Even though we have distilled the sour water somewhat democratically and turned the crap into a welfare sour cream, it is not milk anymore, and we have to be careful that from now on not all roads will lead to Auschwitz. Within fewer years than the number of fingers on one hand, anyone who reads this may be thrown into the fire of his own home. This may be because he can read, for instance, or because he is blond, or for reasons that will not be made clear to him.

Artists and philosophers have been nostalgic for this world of the witnesses for generations, in France no less than in Germany. The French, the admired champions of Latin clarity, have only exercised their torture feasts on people of color in the last one hundred years, and we limit ourselves there to saying "tut tut" until things change. The word *sadism*, preferably used in connection with Germans, is derived from a French proper name.

Even before de Sade, who saw in crime a revelation of the deepest reality, a new underworld came to the surface in Goethe's *Faust*. A little later Jean Paul writes: "A more ingenious and greater revolution than the political one, and only as murderous as this one, is beating in the heart of the world." And shortly thereafter the first, unsharp images of Hitler and his world begin to appear in German romanticism. From the Gothic darkness the face of Coppelius emerges, the "sandman" from the story of the same title by E. T. A. Hoffmann: "an ugly, ghostly monster, who brings in misery, distress, and transitory, eternal destruction everywhere he enters the scene." While in France Lautréamont's Maldoror makes his bulldog maul a girl (a "sacrificial altar"), Nietzsche writes in Germany: "To gain that terrible *energy of greatness*, in order to shape future mankind, through cultivation on the one hand, and through the destruction of millions of failures on the other, and *not to go to pieces* due to the suffering that they *create* and that has never been there before!" Perhaps influenced by this text (but I doubt that), Himmler will say the same thing almost verbatim three quarters of a century later.

Baudelaire has long remarked: "The attractiveness of the horrific only intoxicates the strongest." Thus the portrait sharpens year after year. In 1905, in *Professor Unrat* (later made into the movie *The Blue Angel*), Heinrich Mann describes in detail the future doom of the German intellectual. Later still André Breton, inventor of surrealism, said: "If I obeyed the fiercest and most frequent impulses I feel inside, I would have to walk out into the street with guns in my hands and see what would happen." Only an anti-Semite will maintain that there is a difference between shooting passers-by at random and limiting oneself to passing Jews and Gypsies. At around the same time the German expressionist Arnolt Bronnen stated: "It is better to scream a lot than to be very clever."

Before I continue, I want to make a point of declaring my solidarity with all these authors: from de Sade to Nietzsche and from Hoffmann to Breton, and with the many romanticists, expressionists, Dadaists, surrealists, and futurists I could have mentioned too. I am their colleague. Writing something and doing something makes exactly all the difference in the world. I myself once wrote that I descend from a people "that used to entertain itself by throwing infants into the air and catching them on the points of their sabers"—this does not make me a Nazi, but I am still an author (showing his romantic side). It is important to know how the portrayers of an artistically destroyed world relate to a world destroyer. Whether de Sade and Hoffmann would have marched along is difficult to discern. The first probably would have; the latter would, due to his monstrous appearance, probably have been *abgespritzt* [killed by injection]. I will get to talk about Nietzsche later: he would no doubt have belonged to Hitler's fiercest opponents. One cannot imagine that the expressionists would not have died in the First World War. Brecht and Becher became confirmed anti-Fascists in any case, and party Communists (the latter was secretary of culture in Eastern Germany). The fairly insignificant Bronnen joined the wrong side; of the top names only Gottfried Benn ("*Totenvogel schrein / und die Totenuhren / pochen, bald wird es sein / Nacht und Lemuren*") actually made a few steps across the bloody border toward Hitler.

That the Dadaists and surrealists were integrally reviled by Hitler for being degenerate is telling enough: he, who did with reality what they did with forms, recognized them as his archenemies. Nevertheless, almost all high priests of "Dada, the great destroyer" had trouble with their consciences after the war. In as far as they did not curse Dada or become Catholic, they wrote then that Dadaism was fighting for the personality or about "our great, positive work" (Marcel Janco). The surrealists almost invariably became Marxists, in one form or another, Breton first of all. As a movement, actually only Marinetti's futurism entered Fascism—but that was in Italy. If Hitler had not come with his extermination of the Jews, only a few people would have thought about detesting Mussolini very much; killings of Negroes have never hurt for a long time in Europe.

So it boils down to this: Hitler's world was depicted before its arrival by "opponents." Since they had depicted it, they were in a position to be opponents. Their talent saved them. Less gifted brothers such as Hitler himself could only rid themselves of their nostalgia through actual destruction.

It has often been said that one of the best prophecies of Hitler was not in literature, but in the new German cinema. In 1920 Coppelius appears under the name "Dr. Caligari" in German cinemas. He now has a helper: the medium Cesare, who commits the murders he is ordered to, under hypnosis. When Cesare is finally killed himself, Caligari goes crazy. The same chaotic world of tyranny, revenge, murder, and dangerous theories is seen in Fritz Lang's *Dr. Mabuse* two years later. Mabuse is already the head of a large gang of murderers and counterfeiters. He also hypnotizes, and ends up going crazy in the basement of his house. But in 1922, Hitler's SA was already beating up political opponents; and after the war, when he had perished in the basement of the Reich's Chancellery, the German movie industry topped it off by making a new version of *Dr. Mabuse*, set in a hotel that the SS had built for prominent guests.

Surveying this entire production from E. T. A. Hoffmann to Fritz Lang, one can find them all: from Hitler-Coppelius-Caligari-Mabuse and Himmler-Cesare up to the murdering SS man in Mabuse's gang. But no matter how hard one searches—and I have searched—one person remains missing: Eichmann.

Nobody had thought about him. Not even the greatest genius could imagine him. The calm, dutiful civil servant who hands the girl to Maldoror's bulldog. The calm, dutiful civil servant who hands the surrealist a passer-by to shoot. The calm, dutiful civil servant who holds the student in front of Cesare's knife. The calm, dutiful civil servant who transports the European Jews to Rudolf Höss's gas chambers.

He was no Cesare, who was under "hypnosis," like Himmler. During the interrogations he stated that he was not anti-Semitic, that he had never read the official party literature, and that he read *Mein Kampf* only superficially and not in its entirety. He was not particularly interested in Hitler. He just obeyed. The medium must believe in the hypnotizer, but Eichmann was a medium without belief or hypnosis. Himmler believed in Hitler, but Eichmann only believed in "the order." Himmler would not have believed in anyone else, but Eichmann would have obeyed any other person easily as well. When no more orders came, he immediately changed into a "peaceable citizen," as Servatius so rightly remarked.

He represents the difference between the artist and the murderer. And if I said earlier that objects of art foreshadow future events, then I will say now that Eichmann did not foreshadow anything, because he is not *what* the artists wrote *about*, but *why* they wrote: the new element that they felt was approaching and about which they worried, and that enabled the celluloid Caligari finally to become a true Hitler—a symbol of "progress."

8

$\boxed{6/4/61}$

The Horror and Its Origin

Nazism originated more in certain images than in certain thoughts, I wrote. Perhaps it is useful to examine this claim a little more closely, if we want to find out what kind of "hypnosis" Hitler practiced—and why not on Eichmann—and in what respect Eichmann was the "symbol of progress."

No man with any sense disputes that Marx and Lenin were world-class thinkers. Compared to Hitler, however, even Stalin was a philosophical genius. In the row of names the Nazis used to name their ideological predecessors, Nietzsche's had an honored place. Apart from superficial readers such as the Nazis themselves, this opinion on Nietzsche is only adhered to by Communist and Christian ideologues, who themselves have an interest in discrediting this great mind. The few remaining souls see Nietzsche more as the first *casualty* of Nazism. He knows: "One day the memory of something terrible will be linked to my name—of a crisis that had not existed before on Earth, of the deepest collision of conscience, of a decision invoked against everything that was believed, demanded, and hallowed until that moment." He knows it, but he is not happy about it. "My life now consists in the wish," he writes to his friend Overbeck, "that it might be otherwise with all things than I comprehend, and that somebody might make *my* 'truths' appear incredible to me."*

This truth, which nobody has been able to make implausible, consisted of the realization that God is dead, that the highest values devalue themselves, and that nihilism is nigh: "the most objectionable of all guests." From this follows, among other things, a murderous attack on Christian morals, which man simplifies and turns into a lie. From the ashes rose not so much new morals of the individuals, but morals of the *ranking* of the individuals, with all implications of procreation and violence: the higher one may kill; the lower one must die. Nietzsche said that he had described the history of the next two centuries—seldom has a bold claim proven to be so right. This can be stated, even though we still have a full century to go. But he also said about *The Will to Power*: ". . . I wish I had written it in French, so that it might not appear as reinforcement of some German aspirations."

Such a passage must not have been what Hitler was thinking of when he gave Mussolini Nietzsche's collected works as a present. What could he have thought of a remark such as this one: "The desire for disruption, for change, for becoming, *may* be the expression of the overfully power pregnant with the future . . . ; it may, however, also be the hatred of the failures, of the have-nots, of those who came off badly, that disrupts, must disrupt; this hatred would be provoked and fueled by everything existing, yes, everything that exists, by being itself"? It made Göbbels think of the Jews, in any case. In a speech he made in Prague in November 1940, the phrase comes back in a rotten way: "Like the potato beetle destroys the potato fields, *must* destroy, so the Jew destroys states and peoples." But Nietzsche once wrote: "I will have all anti-Semites shot to death. . . ." From innumerable remarks it appears that he was a confirmed *anti*-anti-Semite, and had he wanted millions of weak and deficient people exterminated, then it would have been the sort that became and always will become Nazis.

*Translation by Walter Kaufmann, ed., *The Portable Nietzsche* (New York: The Viking Press, 1968 [1954]), p. 441.

It is safe to say of Hitler that he hardly read Nietzsche. What Hitler read were at most the anti-Semitic brochures he tells us about in *Mein Kampf*. In the trenches of the First World War he may have read *Thus Spoke Zarathustra*, and Stirner's *The Ego and His Own*—at least my father, who was in the same army, read it then; by the way, my father was, although three years his junior, significantly higher in rank, and Hitler would have had to jump stiffly to attention for him. In my family copy I find the following passage marked: "Tomorrow they carry thee to the grave; soon thy sisters, the peoples, will follow thee. But, when they have all followed, then mankind is buried, and I am my own, I am the laughing heir!"*

It has been pointed out in the past that Hitler was likely to have heard about Nietzsche during his visits to the "Wahnfried" house in Bayreuth: a breeding ground for everything reactionary, and home of the daughters of his idol Richard Wagner, composer of grandiose music, and author of excellent essays such as "Opera and Drama" and exemplary anti-Semitic writings such as "Judaism in Music." But whatever he heard, he did not take over Nietzsche's "thinking," but only the "image" in Nietzsche's work: the *Übermensch*, the merciless *Herrenmensch* on his wispy top, which is exactly the weakest point in all of Nietzsche, who has been unsurpassed in the last one hundred years as cool thinker and sworn enemy of all that is not clear and instinctive, but who scores rather poorly as "depicter," although he also thought that all the greats from history *together* could not have produced even one speech from his *Zarathustra*. But by then he was approaching the psychological darkness that one can call "Hitler," and whose "first casualty" he was.

Hitler took what fit his argument. During the years of the *Kampfzeit*, the shabby, pale young man with his prominent cheekbones and fanatical, bright blue eyes must have heard about other "predecessors" as well. In between the conspiracies and the brawls there was much talking in the beer pubs of Munich by the

*Translated by Steven T. Byington, *The Ego and His Own* (New York: Benj. R. Tucker, 1907), p. 285.

fantastic company surrounding him: fired officers, students on the rocks, degenerate lawyers, reactionary journalists, a former horse trader, a gay wrestler, a bouncer, pimps—who eventually, if they had not been murdered halfway in their power struggle, ended up as cabinet members, generals, viceroys of conquered countries, and later still on the gallows, leaving thirty-five million dead, and Europe in ruins.

They told him about the philosophers of violence, such as the Frenchman Georges Sorel and his theory of the myth preceding action. He heard about "geopolitics" and "Nordic" mythology. Especially one young architect from Estonia told him about the already existing racial doctrine.

This "doctrine" then, about which Rosenberg told him, was in itself already an "image," not a thought. He told him about the French Count Gobineau (Nietzsche perhaps would have done better writing in *English* . . .), who was the first, in the nineteenth century, to design a pseudo-scientific method to explain history from the struggle between qualitatively differing races. Hybridization will be the culture's downfall. "It is not death that arouses our grief, but the certainty that it will only reach us disgraced." Gobineau still bathes everything in feudal melancholy; the emphasis is not on anti-Semitism. This changes with the next one Rosenberg tells him about: Houston Stewart Chamberlain, the son of a British admiral. (Now I've got it: Nietzsche should have written in *Dutch*—no questions would have been asked.) This philosopher was married to a Wagner daughter, Friedelind. Hitler soon got to know him personally at "Wahnfried," and felt excessive admiration. Rosenberg read to Hitler from Chamberlain's *The Foundations of the Nineteenth Century*. In it, the racial doctrine is widened to an aggressive weltanschauung with an extremely anti-Semitic tendency. All the ingredients were already present: the Aryan-German beacon people, the imperialism, Christ not being Jewish, *Kultur*, *Mythos*, *Völkerchaos*, culture, myth, chaos of peoples. Here Rosenberg, who can't stop talking, interrupts and writes his own *The Myth of the Twentieth Century*. It now becomes a demagogical pogrom philosophy, in which Hitler appears as a sort of *Über-Übermensch*, and the normal *SS-Übermensch* obtains the moral legalizing for murder. This in turn produces the screaming voice of Streicher, who does not even pretend to be thinking, but who, already in 1939, screams: "The Jews in Russia must be killed! They must be eradicated root and branch!" And *Judenhetzer Nummer Eins*, Jew Agitator Number One, as he called himself, was still screaming when they hanged him seven years later. He had refused to get dressed, and he had refused to walk; the American MPs dragged him to the gallows in his underwear, while he was screaming: "Heil Hitler! Heil Hitler! Heil Hitler! Heil Hitler!"

And the chatterbox Rosenberg himself? If only he had stuck to talking. As *Reichsminister für die besetzen Ostgebiete* [the Reich's minister for Occupied Eastern Territories] he proceeded to the deeds Streicher had been screaming for. When the noose was put around his neck in Nuremberg, he did not even say he loved Germany, like the others. He did not say anything anymore.

But it would be a big mistake to assume that the origin of the horror lies there. Without Hitler the murderous babbling could have gone on for centuries, resulting at most in a series of pogroms, as they took place throughout the Christian era. Millions of people, now dead, would still be alive. The truth is that Hitler did not need the writing from Gobineau to Rosenberg. He appreciated it as some sort of canonical tradition, which continued next to or behind what he himself possessed, something much more awful: a mystical revelation. He did not need to write or think. *He knew.*

Before the war, the general understanding, which still has adherents today (Hausner, for example), was that the high-ranking Nazi leaders did not believe anything of their doctrine, that they only used it, cynically and demagogically, to achieve their goal of world dominion. Rauschning thought he could even prove it with a statement he recorded from the mouth of Hitler himself: "I know exactly that in the scientific sense there is no such thing as race. As a politician I need a concept that will make it possible to destroy the hitherto historical foundations and to place an entirely new anti-historical order in their stead, and to give this an intellectual basis. With the concept of race, National Socialism can go ahead with its revolution and turn the world upside down."* Rauschning then asks him whether he is planning on exterminating the Jews. "No," says Hitler. "Otherwise we would have to invent them again. It is essential that one has a visible opponent, not just an abstract one."

From then on the Jews were exterminated by the millions, and it was the intention not to leave any one of them visible. It is also not possible to maintain that the popular anger agitated by Hitler himself and by Streicher needed to be satisfied, for the extermination of the Jews was precisely the most secret of all the Reich's plans. Satisfaction was not part of it—apart from a few thousand professional sadists in the camps and in the *Einsatzgruppen* [death squads]; I will discuss the situation with people like Himmler and Eichmann in this respect later. Also Hausner's use of the Hegelian excuse of "the dialectic of the events" and "compulsiveness" falls short.

Rauschning was simply taken for a ride. Hitler thought it was useful to have people abroad think he was only a cynical demagogue: that is, an intelligent man whose bloodlust would turn out not to be so bad—and Rauschning continued telling the world with great success what Hitler wanted it to believe. But it was not easy. The truth was more horrendous. Everything from his doctrine was cynical demagoguery, *except for* the anti-Semitism, yes, *for the sake of* the anti-Semitism. One man was truly satisfied by the killing of the Jews, and that was Hitler.

In order to prove this, we must turn to the passages in *Mein Kampf* in which he describes his development into an anti-Semite—passages that were generally viewed as far-fetched lies after Rauschning's "disclosures"—and of which people say at best today: "It is as though one is stepping into the world of the insane; the Jew is no longer a human being. He has become a mythical figure, a smirking, peeping devil, endowed with hellish powers . . ." (Bullock†). Hellish powers! From where? On those

*Hermann Rauschning, *The Voice of Destruction* (New York: Putnam and Sons, 1940).

†Alan Bullock, *Hitler: A Study in Tyranny* (New York: Odhams Press, 1952).

pages of *Mein Kampf* is the image in which horror finds its origin. For that is how it should be read: from the perspective of the death of innumerable people, and not from the perspective of a fanatical politician, who is writing in prison at age thirty-five.

Let us, just this once, take the führer at his word, just as Rauschning did, and assume that he was indeed sent by a "higher power"—without, neither now nor later, pondering the academic question whether we would perhaps prefer to call that power "psychosis" or "schizophrenia." Then as a resource we will find comparative research on myths, which deals with the construction of schemes that are as generally valid as possible. It is not the most sympathetic science that has set as its task to remove every living and individual thing to end up with a skeleton that could be as much Macchiavelli's or Saint Francis's. Let us follow the path in reverse and dress the skeleton with new organs, flesh, and a face with a small mustache. We will find the framework we need for this in Joseph Campbell's *The Hero with a Thousand Faces*. I have purposely chosen an existing pattern. If I had introduced my own choice of objects to be compared, one could perhaps have criticized me for my prejudice.

Following an impressive show of mythical material of all times and all places, Campbell sets up the carcass of the mythical hero in the final chapter ("The Keys"). There are nine milestones on his way—from his departure from normal life to his return with the captured Elixir, which will save the world. I will link these milestones one at a time to chronological passages from the section on the Jews in the first part of *Mein Kampf*.

Preceding this are pages filled with hatred about Marxism, dragging everything beautiful through the mud, and about Social Democrats, who are just as much traitors of their country. Then Hitler proceeds to disclose the "core," the "true intentions" of Social Democracy. He writes that he had never heard the word "*Jude*" at home, in his father's house in Linz. "I believe that the old gentleman would have regarded any special emphasis on this term as cultural backwardness."* When he was about fifteen, he

---

*Translation by Ralph Manheim, *Mein Kampf by Adolf Hitler* (Boston: Houghton Mifflin Company, 1971 [1943]), p. 51.

often heard the word in school during political conversations: "This filled me with a mild distaste, and I could not rid myself of an unpleasant feeling that always came over me whenever religious quarrels occurred in my presence" [pp. 51–52].

In short: nothing to worry about. An adolescent, less fanatical than most who later trudge toward their retirement.

Then the next sentence: "Then I came to Vienna." Here we have Campbell's first milestone, which he calls "Call to Adventure." The mythical hero leaves his castle—that is, a shabby boy of twenty, with a famished face and hair down to his collar rents a wooden bed in an asylum and earns a living as a dock-worker, snow-clearer, and carpet-beater. Sometimes he sleeps in the park, is deloused, paints postcards, sits in the café, and reads the papers. Which papers?

Also anti-Semitic ones. But he says: "Consequently, the tone, particularly that of the Viennese anti-Semitic press, seemed to me unworthy of the cultural tradition of a great nation. I was oppressed by the memory of certain occurrences in the Middle Ages which I should not have liked to see repeated" [p. 52].

But slowly he is nearing the shadows. Campbell's second milestone emerges: "Helper." "On one such occasion," he writes, "I was forced to recognize that one of the anti-Semitic papers . . . behaved more decently" [p. 54].

Hardly one page later he is on the "Threshold of Adventure," the third milestone, which Campbell specifies with "Brother battle," "Dragon battle," "Dismemberment," "Crucifixion," "Abduction," and "Whale's belly." "My views with regard to anti-Semitism thus succumbed to the passage of time, and this was my greatest transformation of all. It cost me the greatest inner soul struggles, and only after months of battle between my reason and my sentiments did"—nothing less than—"my reason begin to emerge victorious" [p. 55].

I am skipping all the observations that he is bringing in meanwhile about the perversity of the Jews, because there are none. What is happening inside him has nothing to do with *the Jews*. For the process taking place inside him it is immaterial whether his observations are correct or not. His observations are part of the process.

Sometimes doubts are aroused in him, about whether the Jews are really so bad—those are in the fourth milestone, "Tests": "I relapsed for weeks at a time, once even for months" [p. 56]. Not even half a page later the "Helpers" are back, the fifth milestone: "And whatever doubts I may still have nourished were finally dispelled by the attitude of a portion of the Jews themselves" [p. 56].

And then, finally, after yet a lot of squabbling, he finds himself in the deepest of the "Adventure," milestone six, described as: "Sacred marriage," Father atonement," "Apotheosis," and "Elixir theft." He discovers that the Jews control prostitution and the white slave trade, and he writes: "I no longer avoided discussion of the Jewish question; no, now I sought it" [p. 60]. And four lines later he is holding the Elixir in his hands: "When I recognized the Jew as the leader of the Social Democracy, the scales dropped from my eyes. A long soul struggle had reached its conclusion" [p. 60].

Again and again: "soul struggle."

As seventh milestone, "Flight," while he has "ceased to be a weak-kneed cosmopolitan and become an anti-Semite" [p. 64], he studies what he holds for Social Democracy. A little later, on his way back again crossing the "Threshold of Adventure," he has to fight his last struggle: "Just once more—and this was the last time—fearful, oppressive thoughts came to me in profound anguish. When over long periods of human history I scrutinized the activity of the Jewish people, suddenly there rose up in me the fearful question whether inscrutable Destiny, perhaps for reasons unknown to us poor mortals, did not with eternal and immutable resolve, desire the final victory of this little nation" [p. 64].

But he does not hesitate for long on the threshold at milestone eight. Transformed as the mythical hero with spit curl and pluck mustache he enters the world of men, accompanied by an intense vision of fear: "If, with the help of his Marxist creed, the Jew is victorious over the other peoples of the world, his crown will be the funeral wreath of humanity and this planet will, as it did millions of years ago, move through the ether devoid of men" [p. 65].

And in the mystical conscience of the regions where he originated, he shows his Golden Fleece: "Hence today I believe that I am acting in accordance with the will of the Almighty Creator: BY DEFENDING MYSELF AGAINST THE JEW, I AM FIGHTING FOR THE WORK OF THE LORD" [p. 65].

This is the true origin of the horror.

6/11/61

The Order as Fate

This conversion history lasted for two years. If one wants to maintain that the story in *Mein Kampf* is demagoguery (moving from the starting point of a decent man, and then sucking him into anti-Semitism inch by inch), then he is automatically obliged to view Hitler as a talented author: for then the mythical turns I have proven were *created*. This is not borne out by the rest of the book, which is extraordinarily clumsily written. As if that weren't enough, the death of the Jews confirms the fact that he simply wrote the truth, only created his own persona, and was no artist. And even if the story in *Mein Kampf* has been somewhat demagogically enhanced, the same truth is going on behind that lie.

Without assuming Hitler had such a fundamental experience as this one, the origin of the forces with which he turned the German people as crazy as they ended up cannot be explained. For that is what *he* did. Germany was not one of the anti-Semitic countries of old and by nature, like Austria, Hungary, and Poland (where even the *partisans* shot people fleeing Auschwitz [*witness Wells*]). Hitler himself wrote about Germany: "In 1918 there could be no question of a systematic anti-Semitism. I still remember the difficulties one encountered if one so much as uttered the word Jew. Either one was stupidly gaped at, or one experienced the most violent resistance. Our first attempts to show the public

105

the real enemy then seemed almost hopeless. . . ."* Millions of Europeans who know that horses are horses, but who are convinced within twenty years that a certain number of horses are frogs: as an "achievement" this ranks among the most unbelievable ones. And what is more: we are talking about *people* supposedly not being people. These forces do not originate in an anti-Semitism a la "I detest Jews," not in a Viennese anti-Semitism of 1910, but in a horrible revelation of a man without a shade of demagoguery or cynicism when he claims that the "Lord" or "Providence" sent him. Here speaks the deadly seriousness of a natural disaster.

Such a man does not need to read Gobineau or Chamberlain, for the revelation precedes the truth: "In those days I built myself a philosophy and world view, which became the rock hard foundation of my actions at the time. I had very little need for additional learning with what I had created for myself; I did not need to change anything." The revelation that the Jews were guilty is of course exactly the filthiest of all revelations—and *anything* can be revealed!—but its strength does not make that any less. The plague of locusts is as natural as the singing of the nightingale.

What was happening inside Hitler in waltzing Vienna was more catastrophic than any other natural disaster—except maybe for the Flood, which was also more of a revelation than a natural disaster. Never after did he think about anything else. He did not use anti-Semitism to achieve world dominion, but he sought world dominion in order to exterminate the Jews. Against all the advice of his generals, he attacked the Soviet Union: he *could* not adhere to the (cynical) pact with Stalin, which betrayed his most sacred moment; he had to fight the Communists, that is, the Marxists, that is, the Jews. And he ordered a different kind of war from the one in the West: a more merciless and holier war, and the occupied territory immediately fell under Himmler's SS, the percussion instrument of the revelation. When the Russians were already around the corner from the Potsdamer Platz, his last word con-

*Translation by Ralph Manheim, *Mein Kampf by Adolf Hitler* (Boston: Houghton Mifflin Company, 1971 [1943]), pp. 560–561.

cerned the Jews. The final day of bunker life was filled with a last deed, a last official act, a last sacrament, and a last word. The last deed was the killing of his dog—and that is, in his opinion, the only friend man has. The last official act was the sentencing to death of . . . Himmler. The last sacrament was the marrying of his girlfriend. The last word was the end of the "political testament" that he dictated: "Above all, I charge the leaders of the nation and those under them to scrupulous observance of the laws of race and to merciless opposition to the universal poisoner of all peoples, international Jewry."

And a couple of hours later, without friends, he spent the wedding night burning with his bride in the inner court.

The same force that has provided myths their validity throughout time immemorial worked as a persuasive power on people through Hitler "throughout space." This effect is shown by footage of masses brought to a frenzy in the Berlin Sportpalast, including responses such as these: "Weimar! . . . Hitler speaks. About politics, ideas, and organization. Deep and mystical. Almost evangelical. We join him shuddering past the abyss of life. I thank Fate that it gave us this man" (Göbbels, *Tagebuch*, July 6, 1926). Or by a reaction like this one of an opponent: "What I sense now is what one ought to call *holy fear*. I thought I was at a mass meeting, at a political event. *But they are celebrating their worship*. A liturgy is taking place, the grand sacred ceremony of a religion to which I do not belong—and which crushes me and rejects me with much more force than all these terribly tense bodies" (Denis de Rougemont, *Journal d'Allemagne*, 1938). Since the revelation when he was twenty-four, Hitler's eyes had the look that everybody who has seen it once speaks of: from his old brothers-in-arms from the First World War to his general field marshals from the Second. That look meant the death of six million people. Hitler himself never set foot in any extermination camp such as Auschwitz, Sobibor, Treblinka, or Belzec. He did not need to: he was one himself.

Had Hitler suffocated in his crib, no doubt some other newspaper reader would have jumped into the German chaos of the twenties; so too it would have come to an imperialistic war, ending with America and Russia as the new world powers and followed by a liberation of the colonial peoples. But exactly six million fewer people would have died, the Jews. Their death had nothing to do with the war. Hitler took advantage of the dark circumstances the war brought secretly to kill them. (Karl Jaspers remarked in a different context that it is "trivializing" to consider Eichmann a *war* criminal.) Killing the Jews had no connection with "time" or history, but originated directly in the mind of one person.

If it is permissible to schematize here, the killers of the Jews can be divided into three categories. The first category consists of Hitler himself. He celebrated a straight "*sacrifice*" in the sight of the "Lord." It was not even a "human sacrifice," for the revelation said precisely that the sacrifices were not human. He sacrificed animals, yes, beasts: "vermin." (Maybe Streicher is the only one exerting some right to a tiny spot in this first category. He said to the prison psychologist of Nuremberg, Gilbert, that he had not become an anti-Semite due to bad personal experiences or a grudge, but that he had been "called"—not by Hitler, but by "the Talmud." When he wrote that one copulation of an Aryan woman with a Jewish man was enough to poison her blood forever, and that we now know therefore why the Jewish doctor rapes his female patients when they are under anesthesia—then that was the sacred seriousness of a visionary with an IQ of 106.)

Of the second category Himmler is a prime example: the believer. Himmler not only believed everything Hitler said, but probably also most of what Streicher wrote; furthermore, he believed in the most childish by-products of the weltanschauung, such as the "Nordic" mythology, and privately, he also believed in astrology. Without Hitler he would have "detested the Jews" at most, and "smelled them at an hour's distance"—similar to Dutch anti-Semites. But now he even believed in the "runes," and it was his ambition to prove that they were related to the Japanese writing system: thus it would be proven that the Japanese ally was Aryan too. He had "typical" Jews killed carefully and their heads sent in airtight buses to the Institute for Anthropological Research at the University of Strasbourg, where they were to be prepared, measured, and exhibited. Himmler's revelation could only be in Hitler's image. His masseur Felix Kersten said that his pulse shot up to 140 when the führer called to set up an appointment for tea. On August 10, 1942, the former poultry farmer said, with a mouth that always tended to curl up in a smile: "Jews are not people; they are scum, and sympathy for Jews would be misplaced." He meant every word of it, tortured as he was by unbearable stomach cramps. That is why he in no way resembled the colorful lasciviousness of the classic mass murderers, but in everything he resembled the manager of the sanitation department—for he never killed "people."

The latter does not hold true for Eichmann, who represents the most horrifying category. Figures such as Hitler and Himmler, the god and the believer, have appeared before (though never with such a belief, celebrated on such a scale); the "Eichmann" appearance is a first. During the interrogations, which lasted three quarters of a year, Hitler's name was mentioned perhaps only a dozen times. Eichmann could not relate to Hitler's Viennese revelation: "I may, on this occasion—perhaps for the first and also the last time—speak pro domo. I said that I was neither a Jew-hater nor an anti-Semite. That is correct. . . . I said it, I believe, to everybody; everybody heard it once; my men knew it." He read *Mein Kampf* "never in its entirety, and never thoroughly," he did not read Rosenberg's *The Myth*, and as far as the rest is concerned: "I have not actually read any books about National Socialism, neither before nor afterward, at most I have only glanced at or skimmed over them." Just as Hitler viewed Marxism as a Jewish attempt to divert the public's attention, so intelligent people view anti-Semitism as an attempt to divert the attention away from the real problems. Hausner expressed this opinion too, which does not explain the killing of the Jews. And what does Eichmann say? "For Himmler, too, the Jewish Question was also"—this *also* is an important word, referring to the true origin of the murder; Hausner left it out of his citation of this passage—I will start again: "For Himmler, too, the Jewish Question was also a welcome diversion to divert the attention from other tribulations . . . Were there unbearable matters of another nature—then quickly, at least at that time, the Jewish Question was brought up, and the diversion had already happened. Not only Himmler used this tactic, not only the NSDAP branch leaders used this tactic, but also all of the so-called high-ranking officials practiced it." In short, Eichmann is saying the same thing. If he perhaps picked up this theory after the war, then it still points to the absence of anti-Semitism, for once an anti-Semite, always an anti-Semite. Judging by Hitler's revelation, he is the most absolute heretic.

And what *did* this nonbeliever read if he did not read Nazi books? Before he joined the SD he did not read at all, much to the chagrin of his father, he says. "When I was with the SD I did not read these books, but I did start reading other books again; then I read—as I have already been allowed to say in part—the specific Jewish books . . . I could not say even once that in those days I read even—even one other book—let's say novels or something else; I have never read detective tales and I have never read love stories—never in my entire life—up to this very day." In short: he has never read anything in his entire life but Jewish books.

This man did not kill animals, but people. This man took people to the offertory of a heresy he did not believe in. This man is guiltier than the believer, who can (in vain) use his belief as an excuse, that is, the god inside him, who bears his guilt—that is, Hitler. If Eichmann uses his indifference toward Semitism "pro domo," then he passes a much more terrible judgment on himself than one could pass on someone like Himmler. Even if the picture he is giving of himself is not 100 percent truthful (but I do not believe that), then the lie and the way he thinks he can use it in his defense would only serve as yet *another* indicator of the pattern in which his guilt is enclosed.

Eichmann cannot use a god as an excuse, yet he uses something. Something extraordinarily abstract, which may not take away his guilt from him, but it will make it transparent: the "order." One is to "click one's heels together and say 'Yes, sir,' and simply serve." At this moment he *is* saying again and again that he had nothing to do with the gassing, only with the "evacuation," which could be true; and he says that he would admit it if it were so, but it was not, that was a different *Amt*, that was Pohl, that was Höss. He was only the evacuation, and should he pay as an accomplice, that is OK. "If back then I had the guts to say 'Yes, sir,' then today, too, I have the guts to say: 'Please, I am willing—here, my head, is lying on the—there where it belongs,'" but he had nothing to do with the gassing: "Believe me, Captain, I must repeat it once more" that was a different department.

But, luckily, I am not Hausner. I am less concerned with what he has done than with who he is. And so I know from his own words that he would have gassed them if he had received *that* order. Then his name would have simply been Rudolf Höss. Because, says Eichmann, "I obeyed. Whatever they might have ordered me to do, I would have obeyed. Certainly, I would have obeyed. I did obey. I obeyed—I cannot escape from my skin, Captain." Here one cannot be content with an exposé, shaking one's head, about the German obedience-drill education. That solution is a bit too easy, though adhered to by everyone, Eichmann himself above all. More can be said about "an order."

Eichmann followed the priests' orders, which he knew to be false. He would never have given such orders himself, he says (no doubt truthfully), but since he was in a position of *receiving* them, he had to obey them. From this opinion "an order" emerges as something larger than the one giving it and the one receiving it— again as something mystical—as a superhuman power that has to be obeyed, no matter where it is coming from. He was not obsessed with the extermination of the Jews, as Höss says, but he was obsessed with "orders" (just like Höss, by the way). In light of this supernatural conception of "an order"—not from "anti-Semitism"—his behavior in Hungary in 1944 must be understood, when he continued the deportation against the orders from Himmler: Himmler was betraying "an order" (from Hitler). He had become a "renegade," always a possibility with believers. But this is not an option if one does not hold the god inside, but in a word, in "an order," and if one does not care whether it is coming from someone who is a scab, inspired, crazy, or good, and what the order entails—it is there. It is always there. If not Adolf Hitler but Albert Schweitzer had been the Reich's chancellor in those years, and if Eichmann had received an order to transport all sick blacks to modern hospitals, then he would have carried out that order without fail—with the same pleasure in his own promptness as with the work he was now leaving behind. He is less a criminal than he is someone who is capable of anything.

Yes, and there are even signs that Eichmann sabotaged Hitler himself when the latter wanted to let certain Jews escape, for tactical purposes (until the moment of his world dominion). For with that Hitler betrayed his own order, to which he himself was subordinate as well, like Jupiter to "fate": the original one "pronounced" by Jupiter himself. *An order is in effect eternally.* At least, it is in effect as long as the giver of the order is the giver of the order, whoever he is. By betraying his own order, Hitler betrayed Eichmann, who had identified with that ("fatal") order. This is what is going on when Hausner says: "Eichmann was worse than Hitler." Until Hitler's death Eichmann stood by his highest order. After that he became a "peaceable citizen": that is, standing by the order of the society in which he *then* lived. When he was arrested, he stood by the Israeli police and answered all the questions others would not have. In Jerusalem, when the court enters, he is the first one in the room to stand up. Servatius's assistant Wechtenbruch, who talks to him daily, told me that he would jump rope the whole day if they ordered him to jump rope the whole day. He requested the order to hang himself. As long as he does not receive the order, he will not do it, even if his pockets are stuffed with ropes.

This is the "an order is an order" of the third category, which had representatives throughout the SS, as did the second, by the way, the one of the believers—although this group was probably smaller. "An order is an order"—from this formula fate derives the justification for its own existence . . . not unlike Exodus 3:14: "And God said to Moses: 'I am who I am!' And He also said: 'Thus you will say to the children of Israel: I AM has sent me to you.'" But from this we should immediately take away the religious atmosphere that exists between man and his god, even though it is in the shapes of Himmler and Hitler. There is no warmth between man and a word: the cold of steel reigns there. For behind the mystical identification with "an order," which is eternally in effect, something that is extraordinarily unexpected is hiding: technology.

10

6/18/61

The Ideal of Psycho-Technology

"We have become too—I can't find any other way to say it—too much one of the herd . . . Yes, one of the herd, a creature of habit. We are—when we receive an order, we automatically click our heels together and say 'Yes, sir.'"

Automatically. This is the world of machines. If I called Eichmann a "medium without hypnosis" earlier, then that is the definition of a machine. A machine is a rational tool set up to execute any command whatsoever, without comment. The car cannot do anything against the "mystical" command of a foot on the gas. It has no appeals or defense ("To every order that a superior gives, one has to click his heels together and say 'Yes, sir'—there was no second or third option; not at all"). The car has no say in the matter ("An order is not justified; it is communicated—case closed"). It has to obey its fate unconditionally, even if the driver is drunk, insane, or dying—because it is a machine. It lacks an organ to make distinctions. Eichmann sees a philosophical background here: "As the norm I have adhered to the Kantian imperative, and for a long time already." Here he offers the stunning claim that the death trains were rattling to Poland in the name of the categorical imperative, that the crematoriums were roaring in the name of morality.

But I call it the technology—which is precisely not good and not bad, but literally the a-morality. This begs the question: how does a human being, a free individual, change into a machine, into a mechanical executor of orders, into a weapon? The answer is simple: through an oath. "An oath is an oath," says Eichmann. And there it is again: that mysterious formula with which the god in the burning bush revealed himself, just as Aristotle based logic on this axiom: A = A. An oath is the manipulation with which the machine is *organized*. The confession of faith is to the god as the oath of obedience is to the order. The difference is that the oath of obedience contains an element of time: "I will *always* obey"—the confession of faith says: "I believe in God," and not: "I will always believe in God." Those were not the dumbest mystics who, like Angelus Silesius, made the existence of God immediately dependent on the belief in God. Gods can be denied the belief in their existence, that is, their existence can be denied, but orders will keep coming very audibly, whether we believe in them or not, and they keep their inevitability because of the oath sworn once and for all.

It boils down to Eichmann only believing in his own word. This word was God for him, and it made the orders divine. He could not break his word because it was made of iron. It was stronger than the suffering and the deaths of millions of innocent people. Eichmann's credo: my bond is as good as my word. His oath was like a brainwash. He swore it in 1932 (before Himmler in person) in a totally different situation, when there was no talk of exterminating the Jews yet—at least he was definitely not aware of such possibilities. Yet, later there was no escaping the murderous oath once given. That is to say: "I say there is, there was one possible . . . , there was one possibility: take a, a gun and shoot yourself. That is obvious. I did not do that." He puts it simply, and it cannot be denied. Not a few SS men did opt for that possibility, when they realized what their once given vow had led them to—for them there was "*etwas zweites*," ["a second option"]: they had not completely turned into machines yet. Eichmann can only commit suicide if someone *orders* him to (the Israelis, for example). Of his own accord that "*zweites*" will never awaken in him. That is how regrettably amputated he is.

A machine is put together; Eichmann was conceived: that is the difference. In addition to the permanently available option of suicide—but that was an impossibility for him—Eichmann could no more step out of his skin than could a crematorium, which also obeyed its structure. If he derived any pleasure from performing his work, then it was of the same type as the racecar driver in his car, morphing into the machine: the sole of his foot is one with the gas pedal and the engine; his hands are one with the steering wheel and the front wheels. The few times Eichmann feigns enthusiasm, it is the enthusiasm of the record holder: "I will jump into my grave laughing, in the knowledge that five million Jews. . . ." But the racecar driver gets out of his car, becomes a human being again, and at that moment needs the cheering of the stadium. Eichmann can never get out because he is the car himself. That is why he never needed applause. He has never really felt enthusiasm, not because of remorse or disgust, but because a machine does not feel it. A machine does not have emotions such as convictions, not even National Socialist ones. A machine *serves* National Socialists, Communists, Buddhists, and druggists alike. The führer's car is no different from the pope's or the party secretary's. Anyone who can find the ignition can drive it. Wernher Von Braun does not care either whether he is putting together rockets on Peenemünde or at Cape Canaveral—but I am not now comparing Eichmann to Von Braun, but to the rockets.

Years before the war, this "technical" element in National Socialism was noticed by two controversial Germans: Heidegger and Ernst Jünger, but what they did not realize is what kind of man would embody it. They cheered the National Socialists on and made common cause with National Socialism for a while. It is no coincidence that of all the Nazi collaborators precisely these two are still participating in the post-war dialogue: they were the first ones to have *understood* something fundamental about Nazism, albeit with the wrong indication. Words are not adequate to describe the Nazi metaphysical woodcarver Jünger, who sang the praises of the downfall of the mind in technology. I could talk about him for hours. Nobody realized so well (through ecstatic experience, not through cool contemplation) that Nazism was ultimately designed for a self-destruction, in which the entire world would be dragged along. He knew it, and he *loved* it. I, myself, was already convinced during the war that the skull on the hat of the SS man was not so much that of his victim, but his own.

The second German, Heidegger, whose contribution to modern philosophy is significant, reprinted a 1935 lecture in 1953 in which he discusses National Socialism, "with the intrinsic truth and the greatness of the movement." This resulted in a fierce polemic in Germany, which Heidegger had others fight for him. He only declared that the passage would stay put. Following the quoted phrase it says in parentheses: "to wit: with the meeting between technology determined by the planets and modern man." Whether this is what Heidegger means is doubtful—then he could have at least left out the word "greatness." But I don't care what Heidegger means.

Maybe, having come this far, we will now be able to find something of an image of Eichmann in the pre-Nazi literature, the image I looked for in vain a couple of weeks ago. I am not surprised that it can be found in *The Sandman* by E. T. A. Hoffmann: it is the automated doll Olympia, put together by Coppelius and the physics professor Spalanzani. The main character, Nathanael, falls in love with her and the story ends with the two inventors quarreling and breaking the doll to pieces, which drives Nathanael insane. Can we recognize in this beautiful robot the gray SS colonel, just as in Coppelius we clearly see Hitler? "Coppelius is a mean, hostile principle. He can make the horrible happen like a devilish power, which openly came into life, but only if you do not banish him from your senses and thoughts. As long as you believe in him, he *exists* and makes things happen. Your belief is his only power." Olympia cannot escape his power. She does not believe in him, but as a robot she has to obey him. And if we decide that in Olympia we are facing Eichmann, then we suddenly see him in a long tradition: from the many automated musicians and animals (often shown in glass cages) of the eighteenth and seventeenth centuries, to the monasteries of the late Middle Ages: the *Iron Fly* of Regiomontanus, the *Iron Man* of Roger Bacon, the *Artificial Man* of Albertus Magnus, who was allegedly beaten by Thomas

Aquinas with sacred dismay. And farther still: to the *automats* of the Pythagoreans, yes, maybe to the golem from Psalm 139.

The approaching machine—that is why Nietzsche wrote about nihilism. At the same time that the almost eighty-year-old Goethe was worried about the approaching "Mechanical being," he had Mephistopheles supervise the preparation of a "homunculus," an artificial man, in part two of *Faust*. During Nietzsche's life the technology developed into what we know today, only to change the "planet" unrecognizably within a few decades. The danger that machines will change people is not very great. The danger is greater that, together with these new machines, new, altered people will appear too: people like machines, obeying their impulses, without the capability to examine their nature. This is why I called Eichmann "the symbol of progress." This living dead person is the prototype of modern man, who created the machine in his own likeness.

It is dangerous to laugh off as excuses the invocations of "oath" and "order," which typify modern mechanical people like Eichmann. To do so would be another attempt to fit them into a reassuring psychology of the criminal mind, resulting in vigilance falling asleep. We do not have to continue to be wary of criminals; we must continue being wary of perfectly ordinary people. We must keep one eye in the mirror.

Eichmann is no exception. He personifies the perfectly ordinary man, the *"Massentier,"* the *"Gewohnheitstier"* with the mechanical order receptor. But now he has had enough. In a passage he declares decidedly how he thinks he can save himself from this fatal circle: "Today I would not take any more oaths. Today I would—today nobody would get me, no judge would get me to take any sort of witness oath. I reject it. I reject it based on moral grounds." Because it leads to mass murder? Is something stirring in him? Some second or third option? "Because I have the experience how, for example—if you stick to your oath, then you will have to be responsible for the consequences one day . . . For I see it clearly that today one has to account for one's actions because one obeyed due to one's oath. Had I not obeyed at the time, I would have been punished then due to my oath. So, no matter how—how it will end, it is always bad if one somehow had to take an oath. . . ."

The inferiority of this attitude, in which he still can not take his eyes off himself, is the direct consequence of the inferiority of his machine psychology. He cannot imagine that his given "word" does not qualify for *others* as a binding excuse, too. He even expects the Jews to accept it. To make things even more bizarre, he offers a reconciliatory gesture: "I would like to find peace with my former opponents. Maybe that is part of the German character." But this is less part of the German character than of that of the mechanical man, who gave a demonstration of his most terrible possibilities in the Germany of Hitler. In Jerusalem this character is tried in a glass cage, but in all the countries of the world he is a free man, no exceptions, not even Israel, but he has gone unnoticed because no wars were lost, or because no inhumane orders were given.

Eichmann also does not realize that an oath does not have to be taken with so many words in order to be valid. In the more or less civilized Argentinean society, in which he most recently lived, the unspoken order, not under oath, read: be a good citizen, work for a living, do not swear, do not steal, thou shalt not kill, thou shalt work six days—to which should probably be added the commandment of the ex-Nazi central organization: do not get promoted too often, do not get noticed. How well did he abide by these! This is also borne out by his unrivaled correct behavior during the interrogations in Israel. No improper word crossed his lips: "But that is a lie, I have to say. Please forgive me this harsh word," or: "The Final Solution . . . to say it very crassly for once: the killing." He has never called the *act* of killing "crass." Also, when he contradicts people, he constantly apologizes: "That is incorrect, Captain. I am sorry that I have to say this," and then it concerned some order to kill that he had supposedly given. He would *almost* admit it, out of politeness, for *one does not contradict.* When a witness account is read aloud that shows that he shouted when he was drunk that some Jewish pigs were to go to Auschwitz, then he would begin by denying that he said "pigs." Then he would emphasize that he usually did not shout. Third, he would reject the insinuation that he ever showed up drunk for work. Only as a last resort would he fight the allegation that he had the authority to issue deportation orders. Here everything is a lie, except for the last point, probably. For his defense it probably does not make sense to appear to be a decently educated man—one tends to forgive the SS man his scolding and threats—but with this he follows the "order" of the society in which he last lived: behave yourself. He behaves in Israel and Argentina for exactly the same reason that he behaved like an intimidating murderer in Europe: this is what was expected of him. He *is* neither. He is nothing.

This extremely useful, absolutely uncorrupted, highly dangerous man is the precise opposite of a "rebel." He is precisely the opposite of a man who wants to be bad. He is a machine that is good for anything. He is the right man in the right place. He is the ideal of psycho-technology.

Millions like him are roaming the earth. What is the reason citizen X in country Y, for whom there is neither a god nor *etwas drittes*, a third option, does not go to steal and kill, but goes to the office from nine to six? Because his society orders it, and because he has identified with that order. If he is given the order to kill the "enemy," then he will kill the enemy. If he is given the order to eradicate all the redheads, then I would like to see how many, based on *etwas zweites*, a second option, would commit suicide or accept being shot by a firing squad. The A-bomb on Hiroshima, too, which had little or nothing to do with the war, was dutifully dropped by a couple of young men (although the pilot Eatherly later wrote, in a letter to his radar man, Stiborik: "I feel directly responsible and hate myself"). Also, the democratic English police inspector who transported Timothy Evans to the place of execution did not stop to think whether the verdict was fair. He was doing his duty. I do not mean to say: put the pilots, the inspector, and the hangman on trial; if not, release Eichmann (although one could mean it that way: a führer's order in Germany was no less legal than the president's order in the United States and the judicial verdict in England), but I mean: nobody should open *too big* a mouth about it.

I mean: society today is based more on Eichmann than on Chessman.* Chessman did not behave: he was gassed by some "Eichmann" or other—possibly innocently. I mean that thus far the ideologues and believers have determined, in a more or less human fight, what kind of society there will be; the Eichmanns obeyed whoever was the boss then: Hitler, Churchill, Stalin, and Roosevelt. But things may change in the sense (quite a few signs are pointing in that direction) that there will be fewer and fewer Christians, Communists, Socialists, and Nazis, fewer and fewer ideologues and believers, until only the Eichmanns are left in a world of machines. And so the chances are great for the man with the "revelation," who will always be there, to gain absolutely unimaginable power, both for better and for worse.

I mean: it cannot be ruled out that in one hundred years a reporter will research the science fiction literature of our days, for the same reason I look to the literature of the last century.

But what to do with X Eichmann? There is no crematorium in the glass cage—a trial is being held. We will not be satisfied with blowing up or disassembling Eichmann. He differs from a machine in that he was conceived, and not put together, and he differs in the (im-)possibility of suicide. His humanness will show for the last time in his death. As long as there is one other soul on Earth, there will be "an order" for him—he will not be there himself. Today in the Beit Ha'am he is seated behind his documents just like he was seated in the Kurfürstenstraße at the time. He obeys—now it is Judge Landau. His guilty verdict will finally be the *zweites*, second option, that will set his locked-up soul in motion: he has always been a man of words. He is already suffering from heart problems. But he will not find himself until there is no other left, when no more orders come, and he is truly lonesome: in the moment of his death.

As said before, this does not need to be precipitated by an execution.

*Caryl Chessman (1921–1960) was a serial killer, whose fame was based on his ability to extend his execution (in California) by twelve years, and on his publications.

11

6/19–7/2/61

Jerusalem Diary II

Monday, June 19. Over Germany, the Portuguese immigrants are still looking down peevishly; over the Alps, they are beginning to turn around in their seats; over Yugoslavia, they are walking restlessly back and forth through the plane; over Greece, they are all changing places and talking excitedly to each other in Yiddish, and over Rhodes, they are beginning to press their noses against the windows. Darkness has fallen, and somewhat later the coast of Israel appears in the moonlight. The Lockheed begins its descent—as the web of a spider in a fairytale, Tel Aviv is sliding closer. With the smile of a habitué I cede my spot at the small left window. Giving ecstatic cries, refusing to fasten their seatbelts, the travelers are staring down. "Oh, how pretty, how pretty!" The city is no prettier than Lisbon or even Berlin from the air, but it is *their* city: the heavenly Jerusalem almost. Tel Aviv seen from heaven, as once only Adonai saw the cities.

On the concrete, the heat climbs up my pant legs in waves. On the way to Jerusalem everything is becoming increasingly familiar. We even pass a crashed taxi, and I am thinking: there is a German reporter in there, who will later want to sleep in the bed next to mine, but I will avoid that. I choose a hotel with a view of the walls of old Jerusalem, and I ask for a room on one of the upper floors.

Tuesday, June 20. At half past nine, when I am trudging up the steep street to the Beit Ha'am, it must be 85 degrees already. The yellow houses are already shining from the heat now, and every passing bus leaves a hot smolder over the street. Around the courthouse it has become quieter. Patting soldiers and policemen on the back, shaking hands with colleagues and operators, I reach the pressroom, which is half empty, but I am told it was even emptier until yesterday. Everybody is happy to see one another.

Session 75 started an hour ago. Eichmann's face is on the four monitors: he has lost weight and looks older. His facial tics have worsened. Hausner is handing over his last documents. He has not changed. The judges are the same too; only Servatius has put on even more weight perhaps. In the cafeteria, headphones over one ear, we discuss the possibility of Eichmann opening his mouth today. As always during this trial: nobody knows anything. Hausner will probably be done soon, and then Servatius may immediately call on Eichmann as a witness. Everybody agrees that it would be an admission of weakness not to have Eichmann speak.

In the meantime the name of the mysterious Wim Sassen is mentioned through the plastic tube in my ear. Eichmann had conversations with him for months, excerpts of which were published in *Life*. The passage that Hausner is submitting as evidence deals with the Wannsee Conference again, during which the death of the Jews was organized. Eichmann told Sassen that he hung around for a while after the departure of the high-ranking guests, and that he talked with his direct boss Müller, and supreme chief Heydrich. They were seated pleasantly and contentedly by the open fire, and Eichmann saw Heydrich smoke for the first time. In all likelihood, Hausner uses this scene to show that, during this most terrible of all conferences, Eichmann was not the small man he claims to have been. A while later, Hausner hands over his 1,115th and last document, and Landau calls for a brief recess.

The police surveillance has been increased in the room; in the hallways there are policemen too. It is as crowded as on the first day. The two front rows have now officially been reserved for cabinet members, members of Parliament, and other high-ranking officials. Less is seated in the corner, closest to the cage. The next ten rows are occupied by reporters; the remainder of the room, including the balcony, lodges the children of Israel: women with shopping bags, businessmen, bearded believers with black hats, chocolate-brown tanned laborers, and students.

Eichmann appears, and my friend, the court officer, who reportedly still has not fallen off the steps, shouts: "Beit Mishpat!" and in strides the court. Then the following scene plays out, making everybody turn in their seats.

LANDAU (to the court officer, always in Hebrew): "Tell the defendant to stand up." (To Eichmann, who has gotten up,) "You may take off your headphones." (This is because everything the judges, the defendant, and the counsel say to each other is translated by the official translator on the podium.) "Would you like to make a declaration in your defense? If so, then you may do so under oath or not."

EICHMANN: "I wish to do so under oath."

LANDAU: "If you make a declaration under oath, then the public prosecutor or his substitute may cross-examine you."

EICHMANN: "Jawohl."

LANDAU: "You may also not make a declaration at all, and remain silent. So you have three options. Let me repeat these: to make a declaration not under oath, to make a declaration under oath, or to remain silent. Which do you choose?"

EICHMANN: "Declaration under oath."

HAUSNER: "I direct the court's attention to paragraph 5 of the law of the year 1961 concerning the location from which the defendant may give his declaration once he has chosen this path."

LANDAU: "I decide. Decree number 84. Based on paragraph 5 of the law on crimes punishable by death, of the year 1961, I hereby decide that the defendant will make his declaration under oath from the witness stand, for reasons of his own safety. So, now take the New Testament to the defendant" (murmuring in the Old Testament room). "Put your right hand on the Holy Scripture."

EICHMANN: "I do not swear on the Bible, I swear to God, because I am not confessionally bound, but a believer in God." (Agitation in the room; the judges stick their heads together to consult.)

LANDAU: "The court permits you to swear in such a manner that is binding for you."
EICHMANN (sticking two fingers of his right hand up [figure 4]): "I swear to God that my declaration in this court trial will be the truth, the whole truth, and nothing but the truth."

There he is, with his fingers up in the air—he who declared that "on moral grounds" he would never swear again, that no judge would be able to make him, for example, take an oath as a witness, for he had understood that one would then have to bear the consequences. If he had *sworn* then never to swear again, the case would have been a lot clearer now. But apparently he wants to bear the consequences one more time. In the speech that immediately follows, Servatius says that his client is fully aware of what the effect of the cross-examination might be.

It is the fifth time Eichmann takes an oath. The first time was before Himmler, when he joined the SS in 1932: "I swear loyalty and courage to you, Adolf Hitler. I promise obedience to you and to the superiors determined by you, until death. So help me God." The second oath came in the following year, and that was the normal soldiers' oath: "With steel helmet, hand up." He took his third oath in 1934, when he joined the SD. It was renewed in 1939 upon his transfer to the Gestapo: both times an oath of secrecy was added.

If all that he has said about the inevitability of the spoken oath is true, and if my interpretation of it is correct, then it logically follows that he will indeed speak the full truth from now on. Should it become clear that he is lying, then his crimes at the time were not committed due to a miserable loyalty to his word, but because he is a criminal. Should that become clear, then I will tear up my clothes, throw ashes on my head, and say nothing ever again. Until then I will believe him, just as I believe in the death of the six million.

As an explanation for his refusal to swear on the Bible, let me add a quotation from the interrogations for perusal. He says that around 1935 it was fashionable among SS men to leave the church, but he didn't; he was deeply rooted in the Evangelische

Kirche, according to his recollection, and he even got married in church, although they ridiculed him for that. But in subsequent years "I always said to myself: The church—yes. Then is it really possible that the Crucified, who was only human too, and—so—I don't want to elaborate further now—this was—this was my way of thinking." More and more he realized that "it could prove impossible that God is so small that he, here, with the things that are in the Bible, can be seen as the great—as the creator of the universe—as the—the—the Almighty—and then I thought that I had found my own things—I also read Schopenhauer—that the confessional way would be safer, because one was already going up a safe mountain path, and the free road would be dangerous and forever be a road where one had to work alone, and all that—and I said to myself: the God I believe in is bigger than the Christian God, because I believe in a formidable—in a great God, who created the universe and who keeps it in motion, and then I came to a realization, and then I went, in 1937, uninfluenced by no—, influenced by nobody—my wife kept holding me back, but then I quit saying anything at home, since I did not talk about anything work-related with my wife at home anyway—and one day I went to court and had myself deregistered [from the church] and made no further—no use of it, and hardly told anyone a thing."

I will not ruin this amazing quotation by commenting on it. I would only like to point out that this formidable god, who created the universe and who keeps it in motion, was not a "second option" that could break through the SS oath to inhumane obedience. It is therefore by definition an *inhumane* god, a god as pure *force*: the god of machines. It may very well be the same for whom Hitler "fought," for which he "defended himself against the Jew."

To this god he swore in Jerusalem today.

Wednesday, June 21. While the temperature in the city soars to 105 degrees from time to time, it is nice and cool in the courthouse. But even outside the temperature does not really bother people: the mountain air is dry, and at night the temperature drops quickly (as one may recall from the Bible).

Meanwhile Eichmann has returned from invisibility, both in

shape and voice, yesterday and today. He claims he was tied to a bed after his arrest, and that they forced him to certify that he came here of his own free will. He says that the last war was forced upon Germany, and he explains the killing of the Jews by the quick early victories: the Nazis fell prey to exaggerated concepts of invincibility, causing them "to take foolish, senseless, unrestrained measures," which he calls tragic—not for the Jews of course, but for the Germans, who allowed themselves to get carried away by their success. That must be part of the "German character": they were too happy.

One thing becomes clearer with every word: with him we find ourselves in the lowest regions, between the shipwrecks and the reefs. As soon as Landau says something, the most trifling remark, it is as though the sun is rising.

I will not go into the many documents Servatius is submitting, just as I did not do that during Hausner's pleas. The miracle is, by the way, that they are the same. The same documents that are to prove Eichmann's guilt are also used to prove his innocence. That is meaningful enough. Half the time is spent on the meaning of all kinds of signatures, initials, and abbreviations, which bring the translators to the verge of despair. The remainder of the time is filled with Eichmann's administrative lectures about the complicated, extremely obscure structure of the terrorist organization of the Gestapo and the SD, of the relations with each other and with tens of other SS bureaus, the *Einsatzgruppen* [death squads], the party, the departments, the army, and what not; and then in particular again the role of his own Amt IV B4.

If ever form and content were one, then it is when Eichmann is speaking about the hierarchy. It is absolutely incomprehensible. To start with, we are distracted by his voice, which has the intonation of a whip. Probably to leave a good impression on the judges, his speech is even more clipped than on the tapes with Less; also, the Austrian *ei* and the rolling *r* which one remembers from Hitler, are stronger than one suspected at the time. Add to this the terrifying SS jargon, which sidestepped fifteen years of development of the German language, and still his continued inability to say the name "Himmler," for example. When he has to mention

Himmler three times in a sentence, he says, all three times, "*der Reichsführer SS und Chef der deutschen Polizei*"—in one breath, as though it were one single word. (Höss indeed found one word for it in his memoirs: "der RFSSuChddPol.") I would be hard put indeed to find clearer proof that for this man no human relations exist, not then and not now, but only mechanical ones: no human Himmler but "RFSSuChddPol," no Jews but "those who must be killed," and not Eichmann but "I who transported those who must be killed."

Added to the clipped speech is a torrent of words in a baroque syntax I had not thought possible. Parentheses lining up with the next parenthesis. In the fourth parenthesis a sudden reservation with an "on the one hand, but on the other," with a reference to earlier statements, then back to the third parenthesis, taking into consideration the following, with the aim to, in accordance with order such and such, because, although, *Reichsführer SS und Chef der deutschen Polizei*, for, but, by the way, so that, therefore, which does not exclude . . . and so on in an endless roll. He would love to summarize world history since 1933 in one sentence. The extraordinary thing is that he does not seem to have any trouble remembering the thread everybody else lost a long time ago. Never does he hesitate, never is he confused. With resolute movements of his pen he scans the rhythm of the parentheses, demonstrating his incredible memory. It is the lingo of the tax form and of the written record, multiplied to insanity. This way of speaking *is* Fascism.

Meanwhile Landau is listening with a cramped face. Today he cut Eichmann off once. It happened after—or maybe during—a sentence of 250 words (I counted them in the protocol): "I would like to tell the defendant that style is a personal matter; but if he wants us to understand him, and I am also speaking on behalf of my judges, then he will have to use shorter sentences. We know that in German the predicate comes at the end of the sentence, but here it is taking too long until the predicate."

Then Servatius said he, too, had "instructed" his client earlier, but he still had to call Eichmann to order twice in the course of the morning. The all-destroying Accounting Machine cannot be tamed that easily. When he receives an admonition, he jumps to attention like a schoolboy, and says curtly "Jawohl."

Thursday, June 22. Serious gaps are starting to show again in the rows of reporters. With the headphones over their ears, with one eye on the TV, they are in the pressroom beginning their articles.

During the break, I accost Less and go with him to one of the prosecutors' rooms. He is extraordinarily friendly, has a tan skull and an impressive mustache. For almost an entire year he spoke with Eichmann daily for hours on end, and so he knows him better than anybody in Israel. I ask for his personal opinion.

"An opportunist. Herr Eichmann is someone who lets nothing stand in the way of advancing his career. He is a failed engineer with an inferiority complex. That is the reason he developed into some sort of Jewish specialist: to gain the attention of his superiors."

"What do you make of his incessantly pleading the *Befehl* [order]?"

"Ah, of course he is a German first and foremost, but undoubtedly he is also using it as an excuse."

"Do you think he is lying?"

"He is lying. Of course, he is lying."

"If Albert Schweitzer had been chancellor, wouldn't he have served him as well as he served Hitler?"

"Definitely not. Herr Eichmann's organizational skills could only be aroused in a criminal context. He has a clear criminal bent."

"So you view him as a relatively simple psychological case. Don't you think in that way the great lesson of National Socialism is being ignored?"

At this moment the secretary of the prosecutors turns toward her desk.

"I have seen some test for murderers that he underwent. You know: say something about six pictures. Eichmann answered five out of six right, or wrong, depending on how you look at it. There was a remark attached that this was an extreme result: the average murderer only gives two or three of the answers."

I say that I don't attach much value to tests. "Who is to decide that the right answers point to a criminal bent? Maybe they point to something completely different in someone who murdered once. I am pretty sure that I can design a test that will be answered the same by both saints and mass murderers, thus pointing to something they have in common." But just in time I remember that I am here not to answer questions, but to ask them.

"What trait struck you most in Eichmann?"

"Servility."

"Is servility the main trait of a typical murderer?"

Less is laughing. "Perhaps of the German murderer."

"If one did not know his name, would he be likeable or not?"

"I do not know your preference. When he laughs, his eyes don't. He has the eyes of a murderer."

"They say that influenced him positively."

He laughs. The secretary laughs too.

"I was Herr Eichmann's father confessor. One time, with one of the prosecutors present, he said about me, by mistake: 'Herr Dr. Less, my counsel.' After the first few weeks the tic in his face had completely disappeared."

"At this moment it is worse than ever."

"Yes."

"Do you think he will be hanged?"

"I hope so."

In the evening, at a garden party at the Dutch Embassy, Landau and Hausner appear on the lawn too, with their wives. Hausner, without his robe, has again become the small, insignificant man I remember from our lunch. Landau is much taller than I thought: an extraordinary man, who strikes one in a strange, not striking way, even if one does not know him. They give each other friendly nods under the lanterns, but they don't talk to each other.

Friday, June 23. To allow Servatius time to prepare his defense, there are only morning sessions, from half past eight until two. The mush of documents and words was spiced up when Landau addressed Eichmann in German (with a Hebrew accent) for the first time. He admonished him not to digress, and to give short answers to the questions: the questions here in court are intended differently from the police interrogation with Less. Of course he is right, but this makes him lose some of his objectivity, if one recalls that he allowed Hausner's witnesses hours of digressions, which were, although terrible, legally of little relevance. Moreover, no matter how you look at it, *this* witness is in mortal danger, and the others no longer are.

Saturday, June 24. Unspeakably more terrible than the Christian Sunday is the Sabbath. No bus service; no restaurants, cafés, or theaters are open. The Jews are all home lying in bed, sitting in the bathtub, or having a meal. The sun is pounding on a dead city. From the synagogues comes desperate singing. Only some hoodlums, going through the streets, with portable radios and shouting, remind us of human life.

Sunday, June 25. The Beit Ha'am, from where I am sending my text, is deserted like a Dutch school on a Wednesday afternoon. Everybody is at the beach or in one of the swimming pools of the big hotels. In the cafeteria I spend some time talking to Lieutenant Colonel Kopel, one of the leaders of the police force in, on, and around the building: a sturdy, graying man with bright blue eyes and a nose as Germanic as Claudius Civilis's.* Although he emigrated from Germany in 1934, we speak English. He has been in charge of Eichmann since August of last year, and he is not particularly happy about it, although it took Eichmann only one day to figure out the various ranks, and even though a Jewish lieutenant colonel for him is not a Jew but a lieutenant colonel. Kopel thinks he is the type of civil servant in a post office booth. When I tell him that Eichmann's administrative qualities must be superior, he denies that firmly. I find that a healthy attitude: sim-

---

*Gaius Julius Civilis, also known as Claudius Civilis, leader of the Batavian rebellion against the Romans in 69 AD. The reference to his nose probably stems from Rembrandt's painting, *The Conspiracy of Claudius (or Julius) Civilis* (1662).

ply not wanting to hear about any qualities. I ask him whether or not it would be a good move to show Eichmann Israel. He says they did that once with an Egyptian general and his officers, but Eichmann is not good enough for that. Then we have fun with baroque Eichmann expressions. Two nice ones: *"Aktenkundigst"* ["most knowledgeable on documents"], and the discovery of the superlative of *no*: *"in keinster Weise,"* meaning something like: "in the no-est way." Finally the lieutenant colonel tells me that Eichmann wrote a science-fiction novel in Argentina. I could not have gotten a more satisfying piece of information!

Monday, June 26. Eichmann's face is slowly turning into a ruin. No part remains still, the mouth is flying from left to right, the tongue incessantly touches cheeks and lips, the eyes are darting to the sides, a tic is taking hold under the eyes, sometimes on the left, sometimes on the right. The tendency of his head and hands to tremble, something that struck me last month already, has worsened. When his face stiffens from time to time for a moment, it is then cramped into a horrendous grimace.

In the tiresome mishmash of Nazi official relations and responsibilities, to which Eichmann again dedicated his linguistic labyrinths today, there was only one personal moment, at the beginning of the session, and all the journalists were elated: they had their headline. Again it was about the Wannsee Conference of January 20, 1942, to which the trial keeps returning. Even though the four *Einsatzgruppen* had already killed tens of thousands of Jews behind the Eastern front, Heydrich then announced the systematic extermination of *all* European Jews. Eichmann admits that he had prepared the numbers for the speech, though he claims not to have heard of the extermination plan itself until the conference, straight from Heydrich's mouth. How the plans had been worked out is shown by the fact that the British Jews had not been forgotten (330,000), nor the Swiss (18,000), the Swedish (8,000), the Spanish (6,000), the Portuguese (3,000), the Turkish (55,500), and the Irish Jews (4,000). All in all: over 11 million people were to be killed, equaling the population of the Netherlands. Those present were high-ranking officials from all relevant departments and institutions, most of whom had degrees from Europe's most famous universities, and were fathers of promising children.

We can spend a long time thinking about these gentlemen in the pleasure mansion on the lake, a glass of cognac in one hand, an Egyptian cigarette in the other, and their relation to the naked women pressed together, their naked children laid on their heads so as to not waste any gas. Such horrors are easily called "inhumane"—but that would make "humaneness" more a wish than a reality. Animals have never been able even to think up something like this, so "beastly" is the last thing it could be called. Since plants and rocks are not known to have done anything like this either, it is perhaps best to simply to determine that it is typically human. Maybe the hair-raising part of the Wannsee Conference lies in the fact that this humanness revealed itself there in its purest, most abstract form: no victims present, not a drop of blood, solely as a *concept*: groups of gentlemen with a glass of cognac in their hands, surrounded by antique mosaics.

Eichmann hung around to talk with Müller and Heydrich. "You yourself seem to have been very satisfied too," said Servatius this morning. "Could you explain this, please?"

"Yes, sir, only this satisfaction is to be found in a different area than say the Heydrich satisfaction"—and he asks for permission to elaborate on this. His satisfaction had nothing to do with the result of the conference; he was "reassured" since it was not his plan. "Once I could," he says half esoterically, "in a certain way reveal this, my wish to myself—as a result of the Wannsee Conference—at that moment I had sensed a Pilate-like satisfaction in me, since I felt I was guilt-free. Here at the Wannsee Conference only the most prominent of the Reich at the time, the most papal ones, were giving orders; I had to obey and that is what I thought about in all the following years." He adds that his notes written down on the edge of the Argentinean *pampas* confirm this, even when nothing indicated that he would appear before an Israeli court one day.

That was around 1955, in the village of Joaquin Gorina, where he had a rabbit farm. In the quiet there he tried desperately to come to terms with himself. He read non-specialist works about nuclear physics, astronomy, biology, and history; the German weekly *Der Stern* laid its hands on the books: the margins are covered in notes, in which he attempts to justify his past with the text. He also read books about the Nazi era; for example, when he came across a witness statement by Wisliceny mentioning Eichmann, then he wrote in the margin: "unfathomable pig," or "asshole with ears." A German author writing about Eichmann has remarked that he could send hundreds of thousands to a horrible death, harshly but without any sense of hatred, but years after the war he developed a savage hatred toward anyone who touched the basis for his fake justification. Since at least five years before his arrest, he found himself in some sort of crisis, which maybe had something to do with the birth of his Argentinean son Ricardo. This is also when he wrote his autobiography: about eighty pages, of which one copy is in Germany; another in Israel.

"I am slowly getting tired of living as an anonymous traveler between two worlds," he wrote. He accused himself of complicity in murder, and even considered turning himself in to Germany. Since the legal status of a sworn receiver of orders was unclear to him, he gave up that idea. "I was nothing more than a loyal, orderly, correct, and diligent member of the SS and of the Reich's security department, only inspired by idealistic affections toward my native country, which I had the honor of belonging to."

And what about Pilate then, to whom he compared himself this morning? "Without any Pilate-like gesture I state: I am not guilty under the law, nor under my conscience."

Abracadabra-hey presto: then he is there, then he is not! By the way, there is a museum here in Israel showing bars of soap. *Made in Germany* (in English)—from the fat of murdered Jews. This is the kind of soap Pontius Eichmann used to wash his hands.

Tuesday, June 27. I am quickly becoming a real reporter: I can now even offer a world premiere. As one will see in a moment, it may even be called a cosmic premiere. I have succeeded in obtaining a half-hour access to Eichmann's autobiography, which he wrote during his time in prison. So this is a different document from the

Argentinean one I quoted from yesterday. The work is called *Meine Memoiren* and consists of about two hundred handwritten pages. Although Hausner submitted it as evidence, it has thus far not been made public.

For lack of time I had to limit myself to the introduction, which is personal and which interests me most anyway. There too, I had enough trouble with the half-Gothic handwriting, although the writing in itself is clear. As far as I could see the essay itself contained little news; most of it is probably also in the interrogations or will be discussed in the course of the trial.

The first sentence is already clouded in the supernatural: "Today, fifteen years and one day after May 8, 1945, I begin to lead my thoughts back to that nineteenth of March of the year 1906, when at five o'clock in the morning, in Solingen, Rhineland, I entered life on Earth in the shape of a human being."

I will explain what this means. This is a lie. Everything is correct timewise, but there is not a word of truth. He thinks a pensive human being writes this way: it is again not he who is writing— which is an impossibility anyway, since he does not exist. He only exists through others. But in as far as only lies can be his truth (for lack of talent), everything he writes is correct. He is not a real human being, but only takes on the aspect of one. He is a different human being. The administrative pedantry is correct too, as is his focus on May 8, 1945, when his world collapsed.

And the machine writes on. As a child he was "easy to handle and obedient"; obedience was "something indisputable, something that could not be eradicated." His father was for him "the absolute authority." Soon the authority shifted from his father to Hitler. How complete this shift was is shown in a passage from the interrogations, about the same time as this autobiography. He says there that he would have even killed his father if he had received the order to do so.

Otherwise he realizes now that a life defined by "orders, regulations, decrees, and instructions" was, above all, an *easy* life. That is why, when there were no more orders coming after May 8, 1945, he found himself in "an apocalyptic mood." It was as though the Horsemen of the Apocalypse were racing through his head. A thus far unknown life opened up for him, he writes, a life in which he could initially absolutely not find his way. That was his freedom. This was its effect on him: "A black something, square miles in size, bulldozed itself into something else, and appeared to crush my head, to make it to burst; it was knocking against my temples, as with heavy sledgehammers, from the inside out, and I saw all the terrible things that my eyes had to see, from the time when I considered an order to be supreme."

Here he also uses the *language* of the blast furnace because it is not so much a human being in trouble as a whirling machine having lost its engineer. Devoid of the veils of the "order," reality suddenly became *visible*. Hitler was dead and authority lost its holder. Where did it shift to this second time? Whirling, he was suddenly looking for the meaning of life. Until then it had never occurred to him, he writes, that such a question could exist, let alone that he "would dwell upon it." But no matter how he tormented himself during his time as a prisoner of war, under a pseudonym, often together with other desperate SS men, "I could not find a higher meaning for the whole earthly organic and inorganic life."

But finally he could rid himself of his freedom; finally he found a worthy successor for his father and Hitler: "Finally I believed to have recognized in the cosmic MOVEMENT, in the MOVEMENT OF THE UNIVERSE, the one and most original higher meaning of all life." The birth of the god of machines! Last week he swore by this god, who relates to Hitler as Hitler relates to his father—who is mentioned in every daily protocol in Jerusalem: *The Attorney-General of the State of Israel versus Adolf, son of Adolf Karl Eichmann.*

"Now that everything was back in place again, my being could calm down again, because I was not lacking any guidance; I was, like before, led forward." The big hand was once again protectively on the head of the bloody toddler. Everything was "clear, simple, convincing, and making me joyful. . . . When I realized what was happening to me again, I had a high fever, and the camp doctor was taking care of me." Everything from the past had become useless (and perhaps even "invisible" again): "With this recovery, the door of the dark Middle Ages was closed for me, four hundred years later than I had assumed until then." And to show that he does not understand anything, the unfortunate guy asks himself why he did not realize any sooner "that this was the Almighty, that this was the divine force and might in truth." His life would have taken an entirely different course.

And at the end of his novella he calls on the current and future youth to work for peace, although he realizes "that for the dislodging and killing of millions of Germans until now nobody has been punished and surely nobody will ever be punished for it."

Wednesday, June 28. After a morning filled with denials of responsibilities, I walk out of the scorching city to Mount Zion, which immediately borders the walls of Jordanian Jerusalem. In the city, no-man's-land is a strip some hundreds of feet wide, filled with an indescribable ravage of collapsed houses, bullet-ridden streets, and felled trees. Here the rolls of barbed wire lie across arid land, sometimes across an asphalted road, on which no one has set foot for years. If one wanted to try to step on it, one would end up falling down head first and bleeding after taking ten steps: the Arab soldiers, well wrapped up, with red headscarves, are on the rooftops behind their automatic rifles. Through binoculars they are looking at the tourists, who are looking at them through binoculars. Beggars like prophets are wailing and holding out their hands at the foot of the hill of David and Solomon, on which the Lamb one day will be standing with the one hundred four-and-forty thousand. To the right is the steep valley of Gei-Hinnom, where in accordance with the horrors of the heathens, Achaz, the servant of Baal, sacrificed his sons on the altars of the Moloch, just like Manasse later again, who in addition committed sanctimony, paid attention to birds crying, and practiced sorcery. But one day he destroyed his altars—and he destroyed them in a different way from the way the SS destroyed the gas chambers in the Gehenna of Auschwitz, for he converted from a god of motion to a god of limitation: I would not want to claim that the first is "greater" than the latter.

Stairs going up, signs urging respect and head covering, hats for sale here. On the flattened top, with the hot wind from the hills of Judea, some rows of trees offer some shade. The path bends to the left, crosses a yard, and disappears in a complex medieval construction of hallways, inner courts, stairs, and halls. In the scorched niches, bunches of candles are burning for King David. After a lot of searching I find the passage to the Dormitio monastery of the Dominicans, where I know a monk. The priest, who opens the door and hears that I am here for Father Jacob, bares his teeth and says: "Amazing." He apparently learned his English from a textbook for society conversation from 1910.

A little later the monk and I are standing in the crypt in the front of the church, near a fairly horrifying statue of Mary on her deathbed. According to the legend, she fell eternally asleep on this spot, and she ascended, with her body and soul, to heaven. After a walk of about fifty yards, through narrow streets, halls, and hallways, we are in front of the tomb of David: a coffin four meters in length and almost the height of a man, in a dark room that is hardly larger. On benches in a shimmering hall Orthodox people are praying, piously rocking back and forth. If only they knew that Goliath were in that coffin, I am thinking.

We go up some stairs and find ourselves in an empty room, which is not too large and where, according to the Christian tradition, the Last Supper took place; this is also the place where the Holy Ghost is said to have been poured into the apostles. The walls have texts in Arabic: the room served as a mosque for centuries. Now nothing happens here anymore. This is the room for the ritual washing of feet, where Jews, Christians, and Muslims decided on the status quo in the truce of 1948.

Thursday, June 29. In 1944, in Budapest, Eichmann said to the Jewish leader, Joel Brand, that Brand had to fly to the Allies in order to exchange one million Jews for ten thousand trucks: one hundred Jews for one truck. This most insane offer in world history, which failed because nobody wanted the Jews, ruined [Brand's] life. He has graying red hair; his arms are covered in a red glow, too. In the cafeteria he tells me that Eichmann already had that tic with his eyes and his mouth back then. But he was a lot bolder than now. He used only to roar, and the words came out like a machine gun as he stood in the room with his boots spread apart and his hands on his hips. And his orders? He received his orders from the mirror!

An East German journalist interferes in our conversation, asking what on Earth we are talking about. What does it matter how Eichmann was standing in the room; what matters is how today's Eichmanns are standing. The court here, just like the bourgeois press, is only talking about the dead, and about *those* pillars of Fascism that fell together with Hitler, but not about the ones that still exist, such as the big capitalists that brought Hitler to power. Everything that may be displeasing to Bonn is avoided. I say that I would like to agree with him immediately, but that I also know that *Pravda* has recently said the same thing, verbatim, through V. Krimsky, and that it gave a nasty impression to hear the same thing from his mouth with so much personal conviction.

Friday, June 30. The Netherlands is on the agenda. Eichmann rejects any responsibility.

In the afternoon, a gentleman with a hat on gives an hour-long lecture on typical customs in synagogues, in the Artists House. He sings, jumps, sobs, speaks Yiddish, falls forward, hiccups, prays, and the room filled with American tourists is laughing its head off. Tomorrow, he says, tomorrow at six he will give another lecture on the Jews, in the same style. And we all dutifully write down: *Tomorrow at six, funny lecture.* I am almost exploding with annoyance. Take off your hat, I am thinking, go to a kibbutz and do not imitate any Jews. If anything emits the smell of gas, if anything is in contradiction with the State of Israel, then it is this half anti-Semitic romanticism of the filthy, retarded Talmudists, who refuse even to speak Hebrew, naturally refusing the draft, preferring today over tomorrow for the destruction of the state, but they do use the bus system and are kept alive by American Jews, who offer money instead of themselves. But the American Jews are proud of Israel for that. In hotels they ask the waiter where he is from. The poor guy says "Iraq" or "Poland." Then they stare proudly at him, and say with a smile on their faces: "Wonderful."

And then we head for the synagogues! There we go, as loud as we are helpless: women, so thin they seem to be from some underdeveloped nation, with glasses and gold hats a meter in diameter, in pink and yellow dresses, their husbands desperately hobbling behind them, in checkered shirts. Taking pictures and asking dumb questions, we cross the obscure neighborhoods of the believers: two-leveled streets, arched staircases without railings, hallways and trenches in all directions; in every cave there is an old woman, a bearded man of God, and a child with long wool stockings. If you come here with bare arms, you will be heckled; if you smoke a cigarette on the Sabbath, you will be pelted with stones because you are "working." Small wonder that whoever calls this "work" never does any. And this rabbi terror dating back thousands of years reaches into the stratosphere: in a four-engine El-Al Comet Jet, the stewardess is forbidden to serve powdered milk with the coffee if she has just served meat, even over the North Pole.

My goodness! The Persian synagogue: green, for that is the sacred color of Islam; the Spanish synagogue: lit with neon lights like a café; the Yemenite synagogue, with a chair for Elijah strapped to the ceiling, the first El-Al plane. When we are all standing in the Hasidic synagogue, not bigger than a large room, the old rabbi happens to step inside. Well, he just happened to come by, yes, yes, he nods and begins to mumble piously from a book. It is a "kabbalistic" rabbi, says the guide, he knows the Bible by heart. "Oh," the Americans shout. The atmosphere of a kids' party. "Shall I ask him if he wants to bless us?" the guide asks. "Yes!" all the children shout with joy. He goes over to him and something incredible happens: after some absentminded looking up and fending off, the old man stands up and begins to sing, with a broken voice.

When we are outside, a man is passing through the alleys, blowing on a horn with all his might. "That is to signal that the beginning of the Sabbath is in half an hour," says the guide. "We have to go now." A little later I see an old woman coming toward us: she is holding up a large stick, from which a bundle of straw and some pots and pans are hanging. I ask what kind of ritual it is. "Oh, she has been doing this for years," the guide says warily, while taking the borrowed hat off my head. "She is insane."

Saturday, July 1. Sabbath. Worked hard.

Sunday, July 2. Eichmann arrived from Argentina, a year ago, at Lod Airport, from which I am leaving. They boarded him in Argentina in a wheelchair: disguised and under anesthesia. To the police they said, and it was confirmed in his documents, that he was a rich, incurably sick Jew, who wanted to see the land of the fathers one last time before his death.

While I wait for my plane, that image does not leave my brain. The deeper it reaches in me, the greater my emotion. Finally I think of the words a great rabbi once spoke: "He who is forgiving toward the cruel will become cruel toward the forgiving."

12

On Feelings of Guilt, Guilt, and Reality

In the meantime Hausner has finished his cross-examination, and Eichmann has won on points. He turned out to be of greater stature as a defendant than Hausner as a prosecutor. It was actually not planned for the latter to act in that capacity. Some time before the beginning of the trial, Shimron, the much more competent lawyer who was scheduled to do it, caused a deadly accident, for which he was convicted—bad luck that ruled him out, of course. Apart from the fact that Hausner does not have a great personality, is a bad tactician, and a poor orator, his failing is, first and foremost, a result of his fundamental lack of understanding. His knowledge of Nazism is based on books and photographs. We know that he spent days in the world's most horrible museum, Yad Vashem. That is where he must have developed his romantic idea of the Nazis as a pack of savage gangsters who were unrestrained in satisfying their beastly bloodlust. The trial must have taught him now that they were a dull group of godforsaken civil servants doing their godforsaken duty, that Nazism was all much more abstract and insignificant. He told me the first time he saw Eichmann was in the courtroom. The sight of the colorless gas fitter must have intensely surprised him, and the contradiction between his apocalyptic presentation and the shadow in the cage was lost on nobody. Not having the required qualities also made Hausner the only thing he was not allowed to be: a demagogue. He committed the inexcusable mistake of wanting to prove too much—and what I feared during his opening speech has come true: in public opinion, Eichmann has become something like "a man's man after all," and less of a big criminal than was thought. Where did the deducted guilt go? It evaporated into nothingness.

Why on Earth did Hausner want to prove that Eichmann was "worse than Hitler" (even though in a certain sense it was possibly true)? He can't find enough guilt, he is longing for guilt, he loves guilt. As if the one on the lookout is less guilty than the one committing the crime! If he had wanted to prove that Eichmann was an accomplice to mass murder, then he would have gotten the guilty plea from the defendant. It would have sufficed. But still in his closing speech he repeats that Eichmann was like Hitler, and says: "The suffering of those who were killed must be laid at the feet of Adolf Eichmann." But that is the language of the Baal priest! It is a downright *apotheosis*; change the invisible omen, and you have the words of Hitler in August 1961, if he had won the war—at the unveiling of a statue of Eichmann on Mount Zion (for, believe me, such things would have happened then).

Eichmann's sweating, his loss of self-control, his exhaustion, which forced Landau to drop the morning sessions, all of this has little to do with the fear of Hausner's questions, all of which he had anticipated, of course. Something was being done to him that he had never expected: he was being turned into a myth. I do not believe that this has ever happened in world history to someone who was less mythical in character. Not an apotheosis, not a "genesis of a god" would have been right for him, but more an *apocolocynthosis*, which Seneca once dedicated to Emperor Claudius: the "genesis of a pumpkin."

I hope nobody will confuse my words with the language that Klaus Eichmann used in the United States recently. This son of a pumpkin stated that the Jews were only putting the total blame on the little lieutenant colonel because they had not been able to catch a higher officer; if they had not caught his father, they would have blamed a captain; and if they had not been able to catch a captain, they would have blamed a sergeant. What is more, the grapefruit continued, Hitler was urged to kill the Jews by high-ranking Zionists, who needed martyrs. Now we are back to the misunderstood book *Hitler, Créature et Instrument d'Israël, ou Exquisse du plan mondial gigantesque d'Israël pour faire son grand et dernier coup*, which had already appeared in 1938.

As little respect as Eichmann shows for Hausner, he has all the more for the judges—in the order of Halevi, Landau, Raveh, which is also the order as seen from his cage. As far as I have been able to observe, he fears an intelligence in Halevi that is most similar to his own: cunning, reticent, noticing weak spots at first glance, and with a formidable memory, a face like a mask, but eyes that never rest. At the same time he knows that he finds most understanding in Halevi, as shown from questions such as this one, with no confirmation expected, naturally: "You want to appear in the best light with your family. That could create a certain distance between you and the truth. Is that correct?" Or on another occasion: "You may rest assured that the court does not hold any prejudice or grudge against you. We too—like you—are trying to discover the truth. But this requires great moral courage from you. I am not certain you are willing to put your personal safety in second place, in order to discover the truth in its full size."

Halevi has never shown any signs of impatience. This cannot be said of Raveh. When he asks what the defendant actually meant by his philosopher's remark about Kant, he resembles an uncle who throws his body, which has a tendency for listlessness, over the armrest of his chair from time to time, and sighs while listening to the SS response. And in the middle sits the unsurpassed Landau, who will pass a fair judgment, who listens with a serious face when Eichmann calls himself "split," and explains that that is a man who escaped into someone else, as it were: a flight from that part of the character that is led by conscience to the personality bound by duty. Then Landau nods with a serious face and makes a note. As if it matters.

＊　＊　＊

Awaiting Servatius's speech, for which the session has been adjourned for some time, I want to try to describe a couple of notions I have been walking around with since the beginning of this report. On April 21st, I called the trial an artistic creation: a thing both invisible and irrevocable, which the judge is slowly building from the material that is brought in, and that will eventually cause the man under the glass bell to die, or that will leave him alive behind bars.

But, of course, it is exactly the opposite of a work of art—although it is happening here on a stage. For it is not without obligations; it is binding and cannot be changed. It is not the expression of one human being; it is a work of reality forming the basis of man. If the man in the cage is eventually put to death, then it will be with the force and inevitability of a law of nature. Murder is still the expression of a human being: murder is still "artistic"; a death sentence is reality.

I am immensely intrigued by the thinking process with which this reality works. What is going on in the almost bald, attractive head of Moshe Landau? His piece of work has less in common with a work of art than with, for example, a wheel or a semaphore, which are not expressions of a human mind either, but possibilities of nature. Who is Landau? Does it matter who he is? He exists. His place can be taken by someone else. In this he differs from an artist. He is what he is because of the place he occupies, which is not him, but the others: us. That place is reality—and the thinking is not creative but legal. And now a bewildering dance on the table takes place: this thinking has a hold on reality, yes, it *is* reality. I find that more occult than a telekinetic séance or television. If Eichmann is sentenced to death by Landau, it will not be Landau who sentences him, but reality, we, Eichmann himself. This assignment of reality executed by Landau is the opposite of a *Befehl* given by one person. If Landau has Eichmann put to death (and one can already hear that it cannot be formulated in these terms), then he will not be guilty of his death. Not even if it turns out later that Eichmann was innocent. Landau does not have to sign his deed "artistically," like a murderer, for it is not his deed. The responsibility is borne by the place he occupies, that is, again: by reality, by us, by Eichmann himself. (The executioner is a disgusting transitional creature between image and reality, with whom one does not mingle.)

Opposite him is the executioner's helper, Eichmann, who did not carry out sentences, who was not commissioned to kill by reality, but by the order of one person, without wanting it himself, so he says. He does not feel guilty either. He *is* guilty (even if it was proclaimed that a *Führerbefehl* had "*Gesetzeskraft*" ["force of law"]). Thus he is the exact opposite of the innocent fool, who feels guilty although he has *not* killed, but wished he had. Let us not hold Eichmann's absence of feelings of guilt against him. Feelings of guilt are not in reality's domain. According to psychologists the only people who became insane in the concentration camps were those for whom the scenes to which they were exposed were the fulfillment of subconscious desires. Although this proposition cannot be reversed, it is a fact that Eichmann is not insane.

The same legal, "telekinetic" thinking on which the trial is based manifests itself in the State of Israel. Or should I say: in politics? But then not in the politics of the Third Reich, which as an expression of human will was "artistic" and not real: within a couple of years it slipped through Hitler's fingers like water. One could mention Lincoln and Lenin here, but it is most obvious in the State of Israel, which started out with nothing, even without any land or anything like a population—solely with some thoughts in Theodor Herzl's head. Today they are transformed into brand new cities, harbors, roads, cultivated prairies, and over two million people; it must strike every visitor to Israel how much all aspects of his existence have contours and substance, and how tangible they are. Everything that happens *is* something, is irrevocable and influences world events—nothing like the amorphous pulp that characterizes the Netherlands and some other countries that do not exist. Incidentally, Israel will also one day realize its ideals, which boil down to a silting of the access to reality. This silt is called prosperity, contentment. There is no getting around it: the ideal of mankind is the double chin. But only Fascists will then call for "new dynamics." Without a need in reality, only as an expression of a desire, this amounts to a sort of face lift—and the result of that we now know: total petrifaction, with movement only inside the deportation trains.

In another aspect I do not let Hitler intimidate me as much. It is no coincidence that it was the Jews themselves who succeeded in creating a state with empty hands. The Bedouin or Gypsies have not done it. Jews of old have been in a "legal-telekinetic" relation to reality. It is telling that their relation to their god is also of a legal nature regulated by laws and rules: Moses, the Talmud. Never "do they get wrapped up in" their god; they are not in *contact* with God, but in *contract* with God. Their greatest philosopher, Spinoza, philosophized in the form of postulates, propositions, and proofs. The Jewish mind, an outstanding example of nonmystical thought, has resulted in three recent geniuses, who have modified society, nature, and man, respectively, with their laws: Marx, Einstein, and Freud. The common denominator in all of these Jewish "lawmakers" is that they penetrate with the *mind* where it was considered impossible: in those areas that were exactly part of the "mystical" before their actions. This is mathematically opposed to the movement of Hitler's mind.

13

8/20/61

On Common Sense, Christians, and Thomas Mann

End the procedure, close the file, and consider the case closed: with this piece of advice Servatius ended his plea last week, in which he did his duty by challenging the indictment on all counts. Is he expecting much? We know that in custody Eichmann was counting on a trial for historians and a prison sentence of a few years; it is Servatius who first got it into Eichmann's head that a mammoth trial before the forum of the world was awaiting him, probably ending in the death penalty—resulting in Eichmann's first collapse. When one of the judges asked the bulky Rhinelander what he thought should happen to Eichmann if they passed the requested "judgment of Solomon," Servatius laughed and answered that they should launch him in a rocket to the moon. After this he went to pack his suitcases, and the next day he left for Germany, without having talked to Eichmann again.

Apparently they have been arguing, which can still be to Servatius's credit. He has done his job properly. He accused Hausner of Hitlerian methods for declaring someone a criminal without proof. For the German counsel of a Gestapo officer this may go a bit too far, but I am in total agreement with him when he says that because of Hausner's approach the other Nazis are exempted in a weird way and can safely leave their hiding places, for the great guilty party has been found: Adolf Eichmann. He is also right when he states that Hitler, Himmler, and Heydrich appear in a more favorable light after Hausner's argument.

And then this statement: "What was done to the Jews in occupied Europe did not originate in the hearts of human beings. It is the result of political considerations in the brains of the führers." I would like to remark: in all parts of the body, *except for* the brain; and of every nature, *except for* political. He continued that heads of state are responsible, that they have done it in the past and will probably do it in the future again. Here Landau interrupted him: "You were too pessimistic in your last sentence, Dr. Servatius." Then Servatius: "I hope you are right, Mr. President."

And after spending 398 hours in his capsule, Eichmann disappeared in the wall, probably to come back out only for the verdict, which could take a couple of months. Has his soul been put in motion? Is there a human being in the machine after all—as in the amazing chess machine of Freiherr Von Kempelen two hundred years ago? Anyone who has seen Eichmann on TV these last few weeks realizes that he was looking into the face of a man who has practically gone insane. The eyes, the mouth, the entire face is in a constant, shivering, pulling motion, but never does so much as an "expression" form on it. Every separate motion is senseless. No motion is connected to another: the man has been shattered into a thousand pieces. This is emphasized by the total immobility of the rest of his body. That is what happens to a human being who is elevated to the Devil. The motions in his face are not indicative that the horrendousness of his crimes has finally sunk in, but of the fact that nothing is sinking in. Really, this man is being punished. I cannot say that he does not deserve it or that I am delighted. It is hideous, first and foremost.

While we are awaiting the verdict, we are given ample time to ponder the threatening warning Servatius addressed to the Jews: "... *and will probably do it again in the future.*" What optimism made Landau say this was too pessimistic? Twenty years ago, people thought those things were impossible too. What happened

then could happen again. The First World War was no reason for
the Second World War not to take place. Landau's optimism does
not stem from his belief in progress of the human soul, but from
the existence of the State of Israel. There Jews become Israelis, a
people among peoples, changing anti-Semitism into political ag-
gression, which would elicit tanks and bombers as a response. The
Jews outside Israel do not receive the blessing of the head of state,
who, quite understandably, recently denied them the right to call
themselves "Zionists" any longer in America or in the Netherlands. Since the state came into existence, a Jew who is discrimi-
nated against is no longer tragic, but dumb: those who don't want
to come to Israel had better assimilate as quickly as possible and
become invisible. This is the public opinion in Israel. In addition
to many other things, the Eichmann trial is *also* the definitive
dividing line between Jews and Israelis. The latter have once and
for all shown the enormous difference: power and justice against
defenseless slaughter.

But whether it will concern Jews or others—what are we to do
when some painter of postcards once again has a revelation that
this or that group of people must die? What can we do against it?
How will we protect ourselves? With what will we arm ourselves?

Big questions, eliciting only small answers—if at all. They are
preoccupied with a Third World War, which is political, but not
with the possibility of a new offertory, here, there, or someplace
else. Why? Because nothing is pointing toward it? But that is exactly the characteristic of the revelation: that it has no history. All
of a sudden it *is* there—a guest from a different world. It may come
only in a thousand years, but also tomorrow, like the O in roulette.
What will we do then? How will we be protected against ourselves,
if it takes on the shape of a human being again—one who will
naturally not resemble Hitler at all, but who will, for example, be
bald, with a long beard and a fatherly voice? Or young and
healthy, with a compelling, bright look? If he appears in the Krem-
lin, will the Russians then be able to forget the capitalists, and ally
with them to attack him *with* them? If he appears in the White
House, will the Americans and we be able to forget the Communists, and ally with them to destroy him?

I don't believe it one bit. He will seduce the people in his own camp from head to toe, as Hitler did, and not only the head, as Marxism does, or only the stomach, as Capitalism does. They will believe in him, like they believe in a god, and they will be willing to die for him, side-by-side with his victims, finally feeling *alive*. With politics as pretext it will again be

> Ax-time, sword-time,
> shields are sundered,
> wind-time, wolf-time,
> ere the world falls,

as the Edda sings. For nothing has changed.

I am emphatically not speaking of politics, not of war, not of the extermination of enemies, but of the revealed, random striking of the fist, as the Germans exterminated the Jews, and as the Papuans on New Guinea kill twins—the fist that strikes, therefore, particularly in its own camp. The way children are being raised anywhere in the world today hardly holds any guarantees against this. Neither the family nor the school nor any other institution is capable of building a dam of sufficient height against the barbarism. An education as rigorous as that of the Germans, one-sidedly geared toward knowledge and obedience, seemed even to boost it. As far as knowledge is concerned, most members of Eichmann's staff were lawyers; after Heydrich's death the head of the Gestapo, Dr. Kaltenbrunner, was a lawyer too. Eichmann's direct subordinate, the lawyer Dr. Wisliceny, was noticed by the Jews during the war for his quick, bright intellect; the same goes for his judges after the war. The young lawyer Dr. Otto Ohlendorf, as leader of the Einsatzgruppe D [Death Squad D], responsible for ninety thousand deaths, is described as extraordinarily intelligent and highly educated.

The intellect does not offer any guarantee against the revelation—not even its Dutch variety: the "healthy" intellect, that is, common sense. A witty expert on the Dutch national character

(Bomans*) recently drew attention to the innumerable expressions in our language that communicate that one does not feel like doing something, that one is not enthusiastic. When the intelligentsia of this down-to-earth trading nation starts to think, it often boils down to a "not me," "I wouldn't touch it with a ten-foot-pole," "forget it," and "catch me doing that!" Faced with totalitarian barbarism too, this puny prescription is often recommended as an adequate method—as if the grandmaster of this thinking, Menno Ter Braak,† never wrote about "the minimal value of the intellect of intellectuals," and did not commit suicide in 1940. The thinking of his disciples in general does not extend beyond the idea that one must think; and if one researches what his followers think they would eventually place opposite totalitarian barbarism, one finds collective suicide.

For the revelation does not address the intellect, unfortunately. Still talking with his arms covering his head, one has already received a deadly blow below the belt. Therefore, English education seems to be more trustworthy than the German or the Dutch. English education is not primarily focused on obedience, knowledge, or intellect, but on cultivating all sorts of small rules of life, manners, habits, and faces, granted, resulting in English people, but at least not barbarians.

For that matter, it is perhaps not the responsibility of education to form dams against bloody revelations. That is more the job of another revelation. Which one? A moral one such as the Christian revelation did a reasonable job in Germany among small groups of Protestants and Catholics. All in all, it turned out to be worthless. Its fundamental impracticability shows poignantly in Rudolf Höss's account of the Jehovah's Witnesses. When they got to hear their death sentence, "they went almost mad for joy and ecstasy, and they could hardly wait for the day of execution.

*Godfried Bomans (1913–1971), Dutch author of popular, mostly humorous books.

†Menno Ter Braak (1902–1940), Dutch essayist, warning against the Nazi threat in the thirties.

They wrung their hands, gazed enraptured up at the sky, and constantly cried: 'Soon we shall be with Jehovah! How happy we are to have been chosen!' A few days earlier they had witnessed the execution of some of their fellow-believers, and they could hardly be kept under control, so great was their desire to be shot with them. Their frenzy was painful to watch. . . . When their time came, they almost ran to the place of execution. They wished on no account to be bound, for they desired to be able to raise their hands to Jehovah. Transformed by ecstasy, they stood in front of the wooden wall of the rifle-range, seemingly no longer of this world. Thus do I imagine that the first Christian martyrs must have appeared as they waited in the circus for the wild beasts to tear them in pieces. Their faces completely transformed, their eyes raised to heaven, and their hands clasped and lifted in prayer, they went to their death. All who saw them die were deeply moved, and even the execution squad itself was affected."*

In this authentic form, Christianity reveals its impracticability as a defense weapon. In the final analysis, Christians are happy with their deaths, even if it comes to them in the shape of the Nazis. Höss reported that on numerous occasions Himmler set the fanaticism of the Jehovah's Witnesses as an example for the SS. Christians, who are very different from how Höss described them, are of course no Christians, and for the most part they just made common cause with the Nazis. The same goes for the Marxists, who possessed a defense weapon, but only in their *heads*.

This is what the landscape looks like—and, helpless, we are standing in it. Our national indignation this time preserved us from the worst (which does not mean I am trying to justify our wretched attitude in the war); if the revelation arises in our midst next time, we will fare as the Germans did. I believe we need have no illusions about that.

For lack of an effective "counter-revelation," the rest is formed by all sorts of elite concepts, which are, of course, power-

*Translation by Constantine FitzGibbon, in *Commandant of Auschwitz: The Autobiography of Rudolf Hoess* (London: Weidenfeld and Nicolson, 1959), pp. 88–89.

less against the masses who are willing, for some bloodied hands, to give up their freedom *together with* their solitude to the bearer of a revelation. Ter Braak recommended a Dutch version of the English phrase "muddling through" to the European intellectuals: "*schipperen*," "to compromise," a unity through opportunism—"the only unity that is still possible in our culture without romanticism, without *Gleichschaltung*, and without violence as the ultimate reason." His wish was answered.

More militant is the impetus given by Thomas Mann. He understood that one must not coolly and wisely distance oneself from the areas from which the danger is imminent, but, more precisely, one must get in *contact* with the domains below the belt, with the darkness, with the "myth." Subject to abuse in Germany, and "*ausgebürgert*," "stripped of his citizenship"—though not Jewish—wandering from one country to the next, he verbalizes this thought most clearly in correspondence with the Hungarian-Swiss theological historian Karl Kerényi:* "Language's secret is great; the responsibility for this language and its purity is of a symbolic and spiritual nature; it does not in any way have only artistic meaning, but a general, moral meaning. It is responsibility itself, simply human responsibility, including the responsibility for one's own people to keep its image pure in the face of mankind. . . ."

In early 1941 Mann writes from Princeton: "For my part I was happy to see how diligently and cheerfully I can still read, when I am truly in my element—and what should my element be at the time but myth plus psychology. For a long time already I have been a passionate friend of this combination because psychology is actually the means to take away the myth from the shady Fascists, and to 'turn it' into something human. This link represents for me the world of the future, a mankind that is blessed from the mind on down, and 'from the deep that lies beneath.'"

(Of course, by "psychology" he does not mean the lazy way

---

*At this point in the text, Mulisch "use[d this] quotation from Mann to explain why [Mulisch] never translated a German quotation (from Eichmann or Höss)."

of thinking with the quick "explanation," which it has become since Freud fell into the hands of journalists, nurses, and Americans—he means a diving bell, in which one descends to the monsters.)

This post-bourgeois voice is fairly unique, but it has spoken, and perhaps it will prove productive. In any case, Mann was the first to have given a valid depiction of the horror *after* its occurrence. His *Doktor Faustus* is the only book that could penetrate to the core of Nazism, in a tradition that reaches over Goethe's head to Luther, yes, to the Middle Ages, while Nietzsche served as a model for the life of the main character. Mann buffs, who are acquainted with his use of "leitmotivs" throughout his body of work, should look at the similarity between Leverkühn's collapse, his fall off the piano stool, and the death of the hypnotizer Cipolla (Coppelius?) in *Mario and the Magician*, a novella from 1930, which deals with the "Psychology of Fascism," according to the author.

Who knows, maybe one day we will find something that can render the hypnosis of a murder revelation ineffective. But still! What are we to do with the Eichmanns that were never hypnotized? What are we to do with the machines?

14

9/23/61

A Consideration in Warsaw

Following Eichmann's tracks we are led eventually to the final stop of his deportation trains, the scene of the crime. But before going there (with the despicable certainty that I will return), I want to look back over my shoulder at the preceding chapters of this report.

Evening has fallen. Half the city lies outside the window of my room on the tenth floor of the Grand Hotel. I turn off the sound of the TV. The screen shows a barge breaking into two, in a mute hurricane. Across the Weichsel Bridge in the distance, there is a steady flow of traffic. I have been down there. I have seen the city: the old city, its fifteenth-century market, its sixteenth-century Novy Šwiat, the seventeenth century, the eighteenth century, the nineteenth-century Marszalkovska . . . Only after two days of roaming the city did it occur to me that none of the centuries, none of the streets of Warsaw date further back than the second half of the twentieth century.

During the war, the city was slightly less than 100 percent destroyed. It happened in three steps. In 1939, Hitler lashed out for the first time, both on land and through the air. "The categorical, the Prussian imperative seemed to be embodied in steel and armored vehicles, this former compactness, which belongs to the true virtues of our people," wrote Hans Egon Holthusen, entirely in the Nazi Kantian spirit of Eichmann.* With the white sword, the Polish cavalry fought the German philosophy. Halfway through this agony, the Marxist dialectic took on its shape, suddenly—too suddenly, in steel and tanks, and Germany attacked Poland from behind, in accordance with a secret clause of the Hitler-Stalin Pact. Two neighbors like that! We have the Germans and the sea, but they have the Germans and the Russians. Throughout history, their country has been dragged back and forth over the map. Now it even ceased to exist. Stalin and Hitler were dividing it between them, and if the latter had had his way, all Poles would have been exterminated, after which the Dutch people in their entirety would have been deported there to work the land for the Germans, who would have gone swimming in Scheveningen.†

Attacked, betrayed, stabbed in the back, abolished—but still Poland was not lost! In 1943, the Warsaw ghetto rioted—the first Jewish revolt since Bar Kochba's against Hadrian, and the moral basis for the State of Israel. SS General Jürgen Stroop blew the ghetto up, house by house, and he sent Himmler a calligraphic handwritten account of his expedition; those who had not died, fallen, or burned to death were gassed. For the second time an enormous neighborhood vanished. But still Poland was not lost. One year later, the entire population of Warsaw rioted. Children made grenades, women operated mortars . . . Two months later the remainder of the city was destroyed. Two hundred fifty thousand bodies lay among the ruins; three hundred fifty thousand people were taken from Warsaw to concentration camps.

And still Poland was not lost. Totally in ruins, the country found itself again, with six million dead, three million dead Jews. And this inexplicably heroic people—who even in 1956 let a furious Khrushchev wait for hours in an airplane over Warsaw while they released a prisoner tortured by Stalin's secret police and

---

Aufzeichnungen aus dem polnischen Kriege [Remarks from the Polish War]; at this moment, he is one of the best German literary critics.—Author.

†Seaside resort outside The Hague.

named him their leader: Gomulka—this inexplicably heroic people, who made themselves freer *inside* the Soviet Bloc than the Yugoslavs have been able to accomplish outside it, and whose party officials are greeted by Western European Communists with "So, you are from that party of traitors," this inexplicably heroic people, who know that they have to use violence against the Germans, and tricks against the Russians, and not the other way around, as the Hungarians did—these people *renounce* the war.

They have refused to modernize Warsaw as we did with Rotterdam; even brand new, they did not want it to become a monument, not even an upside-down one, to the Germans, or anything to remind them of the war: the city was rebuilt, stone by stone, as it was in 1939. The fifteenth, sixteenth, seventeenth, and eighteenth centuries . . . There is something astonishing in this seamless renunciation of the six-year visit of Zyklon-B philosophers for those who walk the streets of Warsaw: "And that street?" "That one too." "And that square?" "That one too." Only, what I thought to be nineteenth century turned out to be Stalin's neoclassicist non-style, luckily abandoned for years now.

I also visited a vast neighborhood, with some neo-pompous housing blocks, but otherwise innumerable bright, straight apartment buildings, separated by much light and space. Only in the center of this neighborhood were some palace ruins, still to be restored, a reminder (with some boulders in front, in which a couple of yards of rusted tramway rails curved around some weeds) that this was the ghetto. Standing on those boulders, the sole keepers of the past and of the footsteps of those killed, I looked around at the whitewashed silence, it being the universal hallmark of our new, post-Hitler world. It was no less ominous here than in the new neighborhoods of Amsterdam—and I felt again that my true subject was *history*. That is not yet what I felt when I looked at Eichmann in Jerusalem, not yet when I entered East Berlin through the Brandenburg Gate a few months ago; I got that feeling three days ago, when I could only enter East Berlin by U-Bahn since walls had been drawn up everywhere and gun barrels were pointing at each other. A pickup truck drove through the deserted streets, in which boys waving flags were shouting slogans; a while

157

later five, six armored vehicles passed, with motionless boys behind heavy machine guns; later still, a column of five-to-ten-year olds crossed the street, in uniform, waving flags. There were no other passers-by. A boy in a blue uniform was reading on a bench in the sun. The sun was shining.

Eichmann has finally become history. What am I talking about then? People are threatening each other with a destruction that would trivialize the Holocaust, turn it into a memory from the good old days. And no American or Russian will refuse the order to drop bombs on the weak flesh of entire peoples—just as Eichmann did not refuse. What can we hold against Eichmann, now that we are even threatening the unborn, and we have waged that war against our offspring for sixteen years already! But that is no longer called a "war," but a *curse*. Here it is, a man cursing himself, his own children's children. This shows hatred so fundamental that we must still be afraid of having overestimated man. The Russians say whatever they want to, the Americans say whatever they want to, everybody says whatever they want to. When the irreversible happens, it is not "they" who did it, but always we: *we people*. When we think about ourselves, we stare into a sewer into which Dante would not have descended, not even led by a thousand poets.

But I must focus on Eichmann, that was the deal.

The criticism of my articles that fascinates me most is the "tone." It is a criticism from friends; the criticism from others is for others. They say I identify too much with the subject, as much with the accused as with his victims. My trip to his Berlin office has the characteristics of a pilgrimage. And what am I doing there in Auschwitz?

I would like to call a witness. Back in Paris after his stay in Germany, Denis de Rougemont writes in his *Journal d'Allemagne* in March of 1936: "When I try to convey the reason that has revealed 'their' secret to me, and I am doing it with some enthusiasm, then they tell me I am a Hitlerist. That is because people today no longer believe in the wisdom of the mind, but only in the shudders of the intestines. Do not describe mass murder caused by a machine gun in a group of people. Instead of being incensed, they will ask for more details. While they are judging me by their standards, they cannot imagine for a moment that I, having experienced so intensely all that I told them, do not cherish it as they are already cherishing it." And (second witness) Thomas Mann: in 1938 he wrote an excellent piece entitled "Bruder Hitler" ["Brother Hitler"], in which he recognized all the typical qualities of Hitler the artist, by a skunk's standards "an abundantly embarrassing connection."

Of course, this tone has only become more "embarrassing" after Auschwitz than it was in the thirties—but does that make it incorrect? It is the tone of those for whom Auschwitz did not come as a surprise, of those who were right. It is the right tone. What is more: I am not a lawyer or a journalist; I am a writer, the only one to have occupied himself to this extent with Eichmann. I was not invited to write this report, I offered my services myself. The Eichmann case is more about me than I know myself, and this connection goes farther than a thematic link with other work that I have written or will write: together with my work, it points to something I am looking for. Of course I can say: Eichmann is my father. But that is annoying. I will leave that to others. I could also say: he is me. But that is too nice. I can also say: in the trial, the mystery of reality reveals itself. But I have already said that. Now I would like to say: he is one of the two or three people who have changed me.

Above all, he has *cured* me of many things: of indignation without obligation, for example, but also of much carefreeness. He has also taught me a certain vigilance: my eyes have opened a little wider. I see him, myself, as well as others, in a brighter light. What is remarkable here is that the outlines have become more blurred. The boundaries between him and me are lapsing, between the others and him, between me and the others, but also between him and the dead, between the dead and me, between the others and the dead, glitter, straying places . . .

This is where speechlessness begins. I once used the phrase "nuclear psychology," and I would like to repeat it here.

But this language destruction has long since been preceded by a confusion that can only barely be described. An example:

during my stay in Israel I bought an album of folk music, which I played hundreds of times while writing my articles. As a result, this lively Israeli music has become for me not only "the trial," but also "Eichmann," "Auschwitz," gassings, stacks of corpses, children beaten to death, genocide. *And yet, it is still lively Israeli music.* What must I do with the emotion this album still evokes in me? Which kind is it? . . . This confusion is even greater than what Pavlov's dog had to go through, when saliva was filling its mouth upon hearing a bell. So what must the murder of the Jews mean for Eichmann? Linked up with the power, the status, the uniform, the car with chauffeur, the mistresses, the *Schnaps*, the parties, and of course also with the beautiful things he saw: the cities, Budapest, the music he heard, his children—but *naturally* tears come to his eyes, with emotion and nostalgia when thinking back to the days of the gas chambers. How could anyone assume that he would show fear or remorse when hearing the witnesses: those were the good old days. Hausner too will one day recall Eichmann with nostalgia, the days of the trial—and thus the merciless consequence of the horror—for that was *his big time.* And what did camp commandant Höss write when he was transferred from Auschwitz? He had to *tear* himself *loose* "for I had become deeply involved with Auschwitz as a result of all the difficulties and troubles and the many heavy tasks that had been assigned to me there."*

That is what man is like, and he is not very neatly organized. It is possible to hook everything up with everything else inside him. Genocide with cocktail parties, the killing of women with devotion to the Virgin Mary, the killing of children with the love for children. Outside the moral *rules* there is no moral reality anywhere; it does not exist in "human nature." Even that does not exist. It is senseless to say "killing of Jews," just like that. Because one person will shudder, another will gloat, a third one will be moved, a fourth one will shrug his shoulders. For each I first have

---

*Translation by Constantine FitzGibbon, *Commandant of Auschwitz: The Autobiography of Rudolf Hoess* (London: Weidenfeld and Nicolson, 1959), p. 157.

to know in what "force field" the word will land, in what kind of "human nature." Two randomly selected people differ more from each other than lions and lice. In isolation no single word means anything.

Each society, each religion attempts to create a generally valid force field with an ethic to hold the zoo together—and in the case of National Socialism, the killing of the Jews came to mean "solution": something reassuring, something to lift tensions, doubts, and uncertainties, something to be happy about. (Eichmann coined the word.) Inversely, after 1945 "Final Solution" came to mean "mass murder," meaning something terrible—don't get me wrong. Oh, how I would like to claim that this horrible sound of the words "mass murder" (the sound of *our* reality, which in this case is given a voice through Moshe Landau) answers some sort of absolute existential truth. But based on what? It can only be based on a certain *religion*, but not that of the Aztecs, who sacrificed hundreds of thousands. I would like to say: he who cannot believe and therefore cannot believe that mass murder is, in reality, horrible, let him at least *want to* believe it . . . based on nothing.

Man is not a given, but a possibility—for everything. That is of course also his greatness, but that is not our topic. Our topic is the other side of his greatness. Thus Eichmann will not yet again become something great, not an "Anti-Christ" or a "Genghis Khan," but exactly the opposite of "greatness": smallness. Eichmann as the *smallest human being*—with that portrait we are getting closest to the likeness. And he was able to be so small because the technology was so great: the railways, the administration, the gas chambers, the crematoriums.

This small man with his great technology is the one we are fighting. With the arrival of the H-bomb, man has become even smaller—it looks like soon there will nothing left of him to destroy. Here lies the difficulty of our fight against nuclear weapons. We are this technology ourselves, or better: it is what we exactly *no longer* are ourselves; it is our shortcoming, and it is great at our expense. If we fight it in its murderous manifestations, we are fighting ourselves in the first place (there is something contradictory in wanting to own a car and a TV, but then refusing to die from exposure to radiation), and not C or K, who just happen to be sitting at the controls here or there. Using or not using those switches has nothing to do with "politics," nothing with "contrasts" in the world, but these are used simply as a pretext. If tomorrow we all become Communists or entrepreneurs, the threat will still continue unabated—until the end of time because the contrast between ourselves and ourselves will continue. And my mathematical feeling tells me that every possibility will be realized one day, be it tomorrow, be it in a thousand years: Adam and Eve had to eat from the Tree of Knowledge eventually, given the infinite time span, with mathematical certainty—the snake was Time. Eating from the Tree of Matter will signify the "end of time," the "youngest day," exactly as indicated and described with great talent by John on Patmos. The atmosphere in the world, now that we are approaching the year 2000, shows an amazing resemblance to the panic preceding the year 1000.

The *good* side to the existence of nuclear weapons, hardly to be overestimated, is that from now on—for the first time since the Middle Ages—we will have to live with death again. The taboo on death for six centuries has been lifted for good: as in a medieval woodcut, it has danced back into daily life again—and this is precisely the moment for the beginning of a regeneration of man. The taboo on death generated absolute weapons; its lifting might teach us who we are again.

15

9/30/61

A Museum in Oswiecim

On the train from Krakow to Trzebinia, where I transfer to Oswiecim, I delve once more into the events leading to Auschwitz. The sun is rolling along over the woods, over wooden farms and high-voltage installations. In the villages, children wave. Every now and then never-ending freight trains pass.

The first time Jews were linked to gas was in 1924: by Hitler himself. Speaking of the First World War, he wrote in *Mein Kampf* that it would have been good to "just once hold twelve or fifteen thousand of these Hebrew destroyers of our people under poison gas." During the Nuremberg trials, twenty-one years later, the number 5,700,000 was given; 4,194,200 is seen as the lowest possible estimate. Almost 1,000,000 of these died in Auschwitz (in addition to many hundred thousands of Poles, Russians, and Gypsies).

The first gassings took place in Germany, starting in 1939. By 1941, about 60,000 mentally ill, dressed in paper shirts, had been killed by exhaust fumes from engines, in secret, remote institutes. After the German churches raised objections to these killings of Germans, albeit insane ones, the so-called Gemeinnützige Stiftung für Anstaltspflege [Foundation for the General Benefit for Institutional Nursing] could only continue its work with Jews. The

163

churches did not speak up anymore until 1945. The next phase took place behind the Russian front. In the *Einsatzgruppen* [death squads], which were to kill thousands of Polish and Russian Jews there on a daily basis, untenable situations had arisen: the number of suicides among SS men was alarmingly high, many became insane, and all the others became alcoholics. Eichmann observed the mass executions (one time a baby's brains splattered onto his coat, he said in Israel: onto his "field gray-olive green leather coat, lined with bear or lamb fur"), and reported in Berlin that the methods used were inhumane—for the SS personnel, of course. A while later he was able to inspect the first mobile gas chambers. The victims were shoved into the closed platform of a truck, and while the truck was driving, the exhaust was led into the platform. By the time the truck arrived at the mass grave, they had all died. Eichmann accompanied the driver one time, to experience such a trip, but he refused (so he says) to peek through the hatch. This method too, he reported, was unbearable for the men. The next step was taken in the Polish extermination camps of Belzec, Sobibor, and Treblinka: diesel engines blew their carbon monoxide into low stone buildings. Sometimes hundreds of naked people, pressed together, had to wait for hours for their deaths because the engine would not start.

Trzebinia, transfer.

In the buffet I drink a glass of vodka, and on a train I read the name of a small town around here, where my father spent his youth. A little later I am thundering through the abandoned landscape again, across these tracks that the allied forces refused to bomb, in spite of repeated desperate calls from Jewish leaders in Budapest, who had seen Eichmann lead hundreds of thousands to the stations.

In the beginning they only experimented with Zyklon B gassing in extermination camp Majdanek. The camp is close to Lublin, not far from the Russian border. This is where this ill-fated journey took me three days ago. The ambiance was a happy one. Whistling workers were putting tar on the crooked wooden watchtowers, pulling rotten barracks down, and building new ones on the same spot, in accordance with the original German designs.

An old forest ranger, a gun over his shoulder, was watching the scene, a cigarette in his mouth. Groups of tourists were having their pictures taken in front of the big shed, in which the five gas chambers used to be. Inside there were lots of people everywhere. In one of the concrete rooms there was a group of school children. Some were looking with eyebrows raised at the silent walls; most were giggling and pulling on each other's clothes or showing each other their toy cars. One stuck his head through a big hole in the wall. On the other side there was a rusty engine under a roof. It is no use concealing the eyewitness account of Prince Christoph Radziwill, an interned Polish officer: "I will never forget the day the Nazis gassed seventeen hundred Jews in Majdanek, while I was in another section of the camp. That evening many of my fellow Polish prisoners got drunk, to celebrate the day. It is terrible but true." In a barrack turned movie auditorium, the manager of the camp showed me film footage the Russians shot immediately following the liberation. With the horror still on my retina I then saw the crematorium, and the walls covered with names of visitors; the concrete table, used to examine all the bodies' orifices for hidden money or jewelry; the bathtub, with water heated daily by the ovens, used by one of the SS doctors—to prove that he was not afraid. Behind the crematorium, the ditch used to shoot and kill ten thousand people was almost closed again. Cut grass grows over the pyramid of bones and ashes, meters high, meters wide, and dozens of meters long. There was also a small puddle of vomit. One of the children had had too many sweets.

Oswiecim.

Gigantic premises, covered with shunting freight trains, hissing locomotives, lonely cars rolling across a sidetrack and stopping abruptly. The grinding noise spreads throughout the entire train when the locomotive starts its stamping movements. The smoke settles. Everything is black and wet; there is a gray haze in front of the sun. The area around Auschwitz was chosen for its poor water drainage: it is very marshy and has damp, polluted air, a breeding ground for epidemics.

The town is no different from other small Polish towns: calm, poor, unattractive. A taxi takes me to the camp, a five-minute ride.

At a gas station there are some empty school buses. Between the trees some rust-colored buildings are dimly visible. A couple of booths sell books and food. Residential areas now stretch out to very near the camp. Back then, the area was cleared and blocked off, and over ten villages were evacuated.

The crematorium, with its tall, square chimney, stands in front of the entrance: the first thing to greet the prisoner. Inside, every brick of the ovens is adorned with names and dates; on one of the iron carriages used to shove the bodies into the fire lies a wreath of fresh flowers. A door leads to a half-subterranean concrete room of about fifteen by fifty feet: originally the dead body's room. Here the second gassing of Auschwitz took place, a transport of nine hundred Russian prisoners of war. Höss about this: "I must even admit that this gassing set my mind at rest, for the mass extermination of the Jews was to start soon and at that time neither Eichmann nor I was certain how these mass killings were to be carried out. It would be by gas, but we did not know which gas or how it was to be used. Now we had the gas, and we had established a procedure."* The gas was the insecticide Zyklon B, the method consisted of emptying some green cans through the holes in the ceiling. This was done by disinfectors from the health-care department, sitting on the roof, with gas masks on. (A question: are they more or less guilty than Eichmann?) From the crematorium I walk through the gas chamber to the entrance door. Narrow stairs lead upward between plants and undergrowth, and all of a sudden I am face-to-face with rotting gallows. It may be seen as an instrument of the SS, but only one man's life ended here, facing the camp: that of Rudolf Franz Höss. Shortly before that, he realized "that the extermination of the Jews was fundamentally wrong . . . It in no way served the cause of anti-Semitism, but on the contrary, it brought the Jews far closer to their ultimate objective."†

*Translation by Constantine FitzGibbon, *Commandant of Auschwitz: The Autobiography of Rudolf Hoess* (London: Weidenfeld and Nicolson, 1959), p. 147.
†Ibid., p. 178.

The entrance, with the cast iron words ARBEIT MACHT FREI [WORK LIBERATES], is situated on the side of the camp. Watchtowers. Electric barbwire on insulators. In the distance the incessant whistling of trains. The camp is smaller than I had imagined. Three rows of eleven two-story buildings each form a peaceful, albeit somewhat bleak village. Here and there people are strolling. A boy and a girl; the boy has an accordion on his back. In the large camp kitchen they are hammering away and remodeling it. No reality remains anymore of the one hundred thousand killed. The gravel crunches peacefully. Gone are the starved slave laborers; gone are the 12,753,526 reichsmark that I. G. Farben paid to the camp administration. Gone are the executions, the roll calls including dead bodies, while a small string orchestra played, the dogs, the cudgels, the medical experiments, the injections. Block 20 is a building like the others. Yet, there, a certain Stessel personally killed ten thousand people by phenol injections to the heart. We know the names Landru and Christie.* Who knows Stössel? Who knows the name Pánszcyk? He killed twelve thousand people with his own hands. Who knows Rapportführer Gerhard Palitzsch? He personally killed twenty-five thousand people. "Palitzsch was the most cunning and crafty creature I met and experienced throughout my long and varied service in various concentration camps," writes Höss, and that is saying a lot. In the end, he committed a crime, even by German standards: he was punished for a "racial disgrace" with a Jewish woman by transfer to the eastern front, where he reportedly died.

Five buildings have been turned into a museum. Block 11 was the camp's prison; in this prison within a prison there was yet another prison in the basement: the "Bunker." Day and night death sentences were executed, people starved to the point of eating each other, people in bricked up *"Stehzellen"* [standing cells] squeezed together four at a time until they suffocated or became insane. On September 15, 1942, the first gassing took

*Henri Désiré Landru (1869–1922) and John Reginald Christie (1899–1953) were serial killers in France and Great Britain, respectively.

place, in the corridor, after a visit from Eichmann: 600 wounded Russian prisoners of war and 250 sick people from the Auschwitz infirmary were used. But the next morning a fresh can of Zyklon B had to be thrown in because many were still alive.

The four other buildings show remains of the gassed. Thousands of trucks with possessions of the dead rolled to Germany over the years. In honor of the slain Heydrich this undertaking was named Aktion Reinhard. At the end of the war, Auschwitz still had thirty packed warehouses, which the SS tried to burn down. The contents of six warehouses that were spared are on view in the museum. A ten-by-sixty-foot display window with men's shoes. One with women's shoes. With children's shoes. With glasses. With suitcases. With toothbrushes. With tins of shoe polish. With pots and pans. With artificial limbs. With potties. With toys. Everything shabby beyond description: the valuable stuff had been carried away. State of the loot as of June 30, 1943: $261,589.75, 18,766.64 pengö, 236,105 rubles, 25,671 ten-ruble bills, 2,460 kroner, £222,918.60, etc., etc. And also thirty-five carriages with fur coats, 97,581 kilograms of gold coins, 6,640 kilograms of gold chains, 20,952 kilograms of gold wedding rings, 22,740 kilograms of pearls, 11,730 kilograms of gold teeth, 4,148 kilograms of gold watches, etc.

Of course this extremely lucrative industry barely took place in this small camp with one gas chamber. This mother camp did receive delegations from the Red Cross, which would return to Sweden with the report that Auschwitz was, admittedly, a terrible place, but that the rumors about genocide in Auschwitz were unfounded. That is because it took place elsewhere, four miles down the road. But nobody knew anything about that.

At a snack stand outside the camp I have a sausage, drink beer, feel guilty, and walk the road up to Brzezinia, *Birkenau* in German. SS designation: *Auschwitz II*. After fifteen minutes I am offered a ride in an old car with two mechanics, their hands covered in axle grease and oil. They speak only Polish, but are willing to take me there. While we are rushing off, they resume their conversation about the screw that one is holding in his hands. We pass a bridge across a railroad line; it is the bridge on which

Himmler, on March 1, 1941, waved toward where the camp should be built—the camp of the Final Solution decided on in Wannsee. Shortly thereafter, Höss and Eichmann drove in the indicated direction to determine the definitive place.

I see the place.

A gigantic entrance building, with a watchtower above the gate, into which the rails disappear. Hundreds of yards to the left and to the right: barbwire. The mechanics race in. There is not a single soul to be seen. As far as the eye can see: wooden barracks, each separated from the next by more barbwire. To the left of the rails, which separate into three tracks, the barracks have been preserved (the women's camp); to the right much was burned down, leaving stone chimneys in long lines. The cows of the SS had the same barracks, but were provided with a concrete floor and ventilation. The mechanics drive and drive; we will not come back to the same place. At the other end of the camp I see the entrance gate blurred in the mist. It is the loneliest spot on Earth, describable only through silence.

A few hundred feet to the left and right of the end of the tracks: the ruins of two crematoriums blown up by the SS. The ceilings have fallen into the subterranean gas chambers. They are as big as swimming pools. Elevators led to the ovens. Farther down are crematoriums III and IV. The capacity was sixty thousand people a day. Those who could work were selected by a gesture of the hand (this was against Eichmann's wishes: he wanted all Jews to be gassed immediately), until he or she was gassed later anyway due to starvation or illness. Children and old men and women were gassed immediately, as were mothers of children (to spare the SS the separation scenes) and pregnant women. The chimney of one of the crematoriums had cracked from overheating.

Witness Gisa Landau: "When we arrived in Auschwitz in the evening, we were forced to walk to Birkenau. In the distance we saw the sky, red as from a fire. That people would burn this way we could not imagine, although we had been through quite a bit. We did not see any smoke from the chimneys, but a rain of fire. The people asked the guards what was burning there, and they responded that they needed to bake bread, night and day. But we knew that that could not be it."

Höss: "I remember, too, a woman who tried to throw her children out of the gas-chamber, just as the door was closing. Weeping she called out: 'At least let my precious children live.' There were many such shattering scenes, which affected all who witnessed them."*

Witness Krystyna Zywulska: "Now the chimney of crematorium IV, right behind our barracks, started to spit fire. Simultaneously, smoke started to go up from the pit they had dug right next to the crematorium, for this new method—twenty thousand a day. First a thin, gray column of smoke, then thick clouds, eventually eclipsing the sky over this section of the camp. The wind blew the clouds in our direction. They smelled like burning flesh. Similar to when a goose gets burned in the oven, but much stronger. I could hardly breathe. At the same time, a roaring of a thousand voices resounded. 'That is from the pit itself,' said Irene, 'They burn them alive.'"

SS-Obersturmführer Prof. Dr. Johann Kremer (physician; a free man): "September 6. Today, Sunday, excellent lunch: tomato soup, half a chicken with potatoes and red cabbage, dessert, and delicious vanilla ice cream. At eight in the evening again outside for special action (that is, selection for the gas chambers on the platform)—September 23. Tonight at the sixth and seventh special action. Dinner at eight in the evening. There was baked pike, plenty for everyone, real coffee, excellent beer, and sandwiches. —November 8. Tonight participated in two special actions, in rainy, gloomy autumn weather. In the evening a cozy get-together in the camp director's home. There was Bulgarian red wine and Croatian plum schnaps."

Zyklon B consists of light blue pieces of silicon dioxide soaked in a preparation that secretes hydrocyanic acid in a warm and moist environment. That is why the gas chambers were well heated (by the crematoriums) and kept moist (this was automatically the case, due to the hosing away of the blood and excrement

*Translation by FitzGibbon, *Commandant of Auschwitz*, p. 150.

of the previous victims). After a trip of often hundreds of miles in stock cars, the naked prisoners, thinking they were going to be bathed and deloused, arrived to a pleasant atmosphere. Hydrocyanic acid interrupts the release of oxygen in the blood to the cellular tissue; death comes with symptoms of fear and paralysis, and vomiting. They did not always open enough cans. Höss about the normal procedure: "It could be observed through the peep-hole in the door those who were standing nearest to the induction vents were killed at once. It can be said that about one-third died straight away. The remainder staggered about and began to scream and struggle for air. The screaming, however, soon changed to the death rattle and in a few minutes all lay still. After twenty minutes at the latest no movement could be discerned. Those who screamed and those who were old or sick or weak, or the small children, died quicker than those who were healthy or young."* The bodies lay mostly near the doors, in a contorted posture, their eyes wide open, and blood coming out of their noses.

Zyklon B was supplied by the companies of Degesch and Testa, of the I. G. Farben Konzern. In the year 1943 they supplied 12,174.09 kilograms, on which the net profit was 127,985.79 reichsmark. The crematoriums were supplied by the company of J. A. Topf & Söhne in Wiesbaden. On January 5, 1953, this company obtained patent no. 861731 for a "treatment and processing for the burning of corpses, cadavers, and parts thereof."

And in the white mist the sun of Birkenau is hanging. In the distance the locomotives are still steadily blowing their whistles.

*Ibid., p. 198.

INDEX

INDEX

INDEX

INDEX

INDEX